FLYING HAWAII
A PILOT'S GUIDE TO THE ISLANDS
BY PETER N. FORMAN

Barnstormer Books

P.O. Box 6893
Reno, NV. 89513
www.wecanfly.com

Cover Photo: Amy Hughes banks her Cessna 152 around Kaena Point, the Westernmost tip of Oahu. Photo by Tamra Brown.

SECOND EDITION

Copyright © 2000 by Barnstormer Books

Printed in the United States of America

ISBN 0-9701594-0-4

For Tamra
Me Ke Aloha

Update Your Guide

How can you ensure that your copy of *FLYING HAWAII* is up to date? Visit our web site, of course. Information on FBOs, airports and procedures is certain to change. Additional information and internet links will also be included.

www.wecanfly.com/flyhi

Contents

Introduction   vii

1 **Before You Leave Home**   1
   Your Flight: Transportation or Touring—Scheduling Your
   Checkout and Trip—Documents to Bring with You—Other
   Items to Bring—Figuring Trip Costs—Techniques to Brush
   Up on

2 **Island Weather**   7
   Trade Wind Conditions—Kona Wind Conditions—Visibility—
   Flying IFR—Severe Weather—Turbulence—Pilot Weather
   Services

3 **Cross-Country Flight Preparations**   17
   Island Reporting Flight Plans—Cruising Altitudes at or
   Below 3000 Ft.—North Shores vs. South Shores—
   Recommended Time of Day for Flights—Overwater
   Navigation—Lost Procedures—Enroute Traffic Avoidance

4 **Safety Procedures**   25
   Equipment—Ditching—Until Help Arrives—Statistics—
   Forced Landings—Terrain Avoidance

5 **Flying from Honolulu International and Kalaeloa**   35
   Class B Airspace—Airport Procedures—VFR Approach and
   Departure Routes—Avoiding Common Mistakes—Your
   Checkout Flight—Kalaeloa Airport Information & Diagrams

6 Around Oahu 47
Honolulu—Honolulu Harbor—Punchbowl and Diamond
Head—Eastern Oahu—Koolau Mountains—Windward
Oahu—North Shore Oahu—Central Valley—Dillingham
Airfield—Waianaie Coast—Pearl Harbor

7 Molokai and Lanai 59
Kepuhi Beach—Kalaupapa Peninsula—North Shore
Molokai—Kahiwa Falls—Cape Halawa—Elephant Rock—
East Molokai Fish Ponds—Lanai—Lanai City

8 Maui 69
Nakalele Point—West Maui Mountains—Central Valley—
Haleakala—Hana Highway—Keanae Peninsula—Hana—
Kahoolawe—Molokini—Lahaina—Kaanapali—Thar She Blows!

9 Hawaii, The Big Island 83
Parker Ranch—Mauna Kea—Kona Coast—Kealakekua
Bay—South Point—The Volcanoes—Hilo—Akaka Falls—
Hamakua Coast—Waipio Valley

10 Kauai 101
Enroute Traffic—Poipu Beach Area—Waimea—Niihau—
Leeward Islands—Waimea Canyon—Mt. Waialeale—Na
Pali Coastline—Hanalei Bay—Princeville—Wailua River
Waterfalls

Appendix A Hawaiian Airports 113

Appendix B FBOs, Frequencies, etc. 129

Appendix C Exotic Air Adventures 137

Appendix D Pronouncing Hawaiian Place Names 143

Glossary 147

Index 149

Introduction

Aloha. How better can the beauty of the Hawaiian Islands be seen than from aloft? Through the windows of your light plane you can view unspoiled scenery that few visitors ever see. Take a flight over Hawaii and look down the steaming throat of an active volcano. Fly offshore the cliffs of Molokai's north shore after a rainstorm and watch hundreds of waterfalls cascading to the sea (rainbows are often included at no extra charge). These islands offer some of the most exotic scenery to be found anywhere in the world.

To get the most from your flight you'll want to know as much about Hawaiian flying as possible, and that's the purpose of this book. Its contents are directed towards both visiting pilots and residents as well. The first chapters expose common misconceptions about flying in Hawaii and present information that will help you plan a safe flight. Appendix A contains photos and descriptions of fourteen civil airports. The book includes a guide to viewing each island's most impressive points of interest.

If you don't already know which islands you'd like to include in your flight, take a look at Chapters 6 through 10. Browse through photos of waterfalls, rain forests, volcanoes, and historical sites, and pick the type of scenery that most appeals to you. Each island has its own character, and before long you'll be able to select your favorites.

Much can be learned from pilots who fly among the islands for a living, especially commuter airline pilots and air tour pilots. Seldom, though, do recreational pilots have the opportunity to pick up ideas from these professionals. My aim in writing this book has been to assemble the tricks-of-the-trade used by various groups of pilots and make this information available to anyone who is interested.

If you've never before flown in Hawaii, consider this your invitation. Weather is usually acceptable for touring flights throughout the year, and a wide variety of rental planes is always available. A flight among the Hawaiian Islands will surely be one of the highlights of your flying career.

Chapter 1
Before You Leave Home

Each year, employees at fixed base operations in Honolulu see the same predictable events. In summer the trade winds blow with a good amount of enthusiasm; in fall they subside a bit. During the winter months, numerous cumulus clouds on the nearby Koolau Mountains drop more rain than usual. In early spring, pilots returning from cross-country flights talk about the whales they spotted enroute.

No matter what time of year, though, visiting pilots who come to these FBOs to rent planes show up with the same misconceptions about flying in Hawaii and encounter the same problems caused by improper preparations. The consequences of these misconceptions and inadequate preparations range from minor inconveniences to trip cancellations. Information in this chapter should help you avoid many common planning errors.

YOUR FLIGHT: TRANSPORTATION OR TOURING

Should you use a light plane as a means of transportation between one vacation spot and the next, or should sightseeing be the primary goal of your flight? Here are a few ideas to help you decide.

Unless you can borrow your company Falcon 50 or Gulfstream G-5, you'll probably arrive in Hawaii aboard an airliner. Therefore, you'll need to rent a plane for your personal flying among the islands.

Rental planes have a major drawback for use as transportation vehicles: The minimum flight time per day requirement. Fixed base operators in Hawaii will require that several hours of revenue be brought in for an airplane every day that it's away from home base.

If you keep the plane and don't fly these hours, you pay for them anyway. There are usually exceptions to this rule, though, such as when bad weather delays the return of a plane.

With a bit of creativity you can work around the minimum hours per day rule. One common technique is to use the plane exclusively as a touring vehicle. Depart in the morning, spend the day viewing the island or islands of your choice, and return that afternoon. The islands are reasonably close together and you can see much in one day. Rental planes are available not only at Honolulu International but also at airports on Maui and Hawaii. If your vacation plans include a stay on one of these neighbor islands, you can enjoy the luxury of basing your touring flight from an airport with relatively light traffic.

When a light plane is to be used as round-trip transportation for a vacation trip to another island, the minimum flight time per day rule will likely determine the length of stay. You can sometimes stretch the length of stay through careful planning. Take a look at Appendix B in the back of this book to find out which FBOs offer the most attractive minimum flight time requirements. You can occasionally negotiate an aircraft rental with less than the regular minimum time requirements if the proposed flight is a long one and business is slow at the FBO. In any event, the sooner you discuss your plans with the management of your chosen FBO, the sooner you'll be able to organize the rest of your vacation plans.

Here is a third technique for blending a light plane flight into your vacation plans. Suppose that you and your friends plan to spend a week on Maui, and you feel that the expense of renting a plane would be justified only if the plane provided some of your needed transportation between Honolulu and Maui. In this case, consider using the plane for one-way transportation. Depart Honolulu, tour the islands of Molokai and Maui, and drop your passengers off on Maui before returning the plane. You then have to take an airliner from Honolulu to Maui, but one ticket costs a lot less than four. Chances are that you'll need to transport much of your party's luggage on the airliner, and you should be prepared to pay excess baggage charges.

SCHEDULING YOUR CHECKOUT AND TRIP

With a five-minute phone call to Hawaii, you can schedule a checkout flight and reserve a plane for your trip. Make sure, though, that you consider some of the finer points in trip planning before placing the call.

If your proposed flight is to originate in Honolulu, are you prepared for operating from a busy tower-controlled field? Few airports in the country handle as much jumbo jet traffic as Honolulu International, and during daylight hours this airport is a beehive of activity. To determine whether your background has prepared you for flying from Honolulu International, ask yourself this question: "Can I communicate quickly and clearly over the radio?" If your answer is "yes," chances are you'll encounter no serious problems. Flying experience from major jet airports is not a necessary prerequisite for checking out from Honolulu International, but an ability to communicate well over the radio is essential. A solid knowledge of wake turbulence avoidance is also needed. If you're in doubt about your ability to fly from Honolulu International, plan to rent your plane at an airport on another island.

If possible, avoid scheduling your checkout flight and your trip to take place on the same day. You're bound to learn a few things about flying in Hawaii during the actual checkout and ground session, and your trip will likely run smoother if you've had time to assimilate the new information.

A touring flight is best scheduled to occur near the beginning of a stay on an island. That way, if the flight must be canceled due to weather, it can be rescheduled for a later date. We tend to picture Hawaii as always being blessed with blue sky and sunshine, but even this paradise sees its share of rainy days.

Once you've decided on the details of your flight, you can make that phone call to schedule your checkout and trip. How far in advance should your call be made? If you try to reserve a plane more than two months ahead of time, there's a good chance the FBO's scheduler will not yet have prepared a schedule covering the date you're requesting, and she'll ask you to call back later. If you make your call less than a month ahead of time, you run the risk of discovering that the plane you wish to rent has already been reserved by someone else. Therefore, a call between one and two months before your desired date will be your best bet. Just as with an airline, you should call the FBO a week or two before your trip to reconfirm your reservation.

DOCUMENTS TO BRING WITH YOU

You'll need to produce the proper paperwork in order to rent a plane. Fixed base operators in Hawaii are known for being thorough in their inspections of your qualifications. In fact, some operators even make photocopies of your paperwork. Listed below are those documents you'll need to bring with you.

- Pilot Certificate.
- FCC Radio License.
- Medical Certificate— Ensure that your medical will not have expired.
- Logbooks— You should bring your pilot logbooks with you to Hawaii, especially if you plan to rent a twin-engine plane or a complex single. Insurance companies list specific pilot experience minimums for many of the planes that they insure, and your logbooks may be needed to show that you meet the requirements.
- Proof of recent Biennial Flight Review (BFR)— You'll need to show that within the past 24 months you have satisfied the requirements of a flight review, as spelled out in FAR Part 61. A logbook with the proper BFR endorsement made by a flight instructor is acceptable. A separate document with the same endorsement would also be acceptable. If the date of issue of your pilot certificate is less than two years old, the certificate itself satisfies the requirement.

OTHER ITEMS TO BRING

Here is a list of items that aren't necessary for a safe flight but are nice to have along anyway.

- ☐ Camera and film— If you have even the slightest interest in photography, bring your camera and plenty of color film. Hawaii surely rates as one of the finest locations in the world for aerial photography, and once airborne you will realize that the effort to bring photo equipment was well worth it.

  Consider the effect of the air's salt content while planning your photos, though. Humid, salt-laden air found at low altitudes in Hawaii typically restricts visibility to about twenty miles, and photos taken of objects many miles away are likely to turn out hazy. This problem can be avoided. One obvious solution is to restrict photos to those scenes that are close enough to appear clear to the naked eye. Another technique is to climb above the haze layer. Its top usually coincides with the top of the lowest cloud layer, and visibility improves dramatically once you're above that altitude. Photos of distant subjects such as the Big Island's snow-capped mountains become possible when taken through high-altitude air. A third technique simply involves shooting on one of those rare days when visibility is excellent at all altitudes. Chapter 2 describes when such days are most likely to occur. Finally, a polarizer filter can help reduce the haze effect.

☐ Compact luggage— If an overnight stop will be included in you tour, remember to bring some luggage which is small or collapsible enough to fit into a light plane's luggage compartment.

☐ Portable stereo tape player— Pack up the Sony Walkman or whatever headphone-equipped tape player you own and bring it with you. Hawaii's scenery was somehow meant to be viewed with music, and the right tunes can add a special flavor to the flight. You might enjoy picking up a cassette of Hawaiian music. After returning home, you'll discover how visions of the island return whenever the music is replayed. A tape player will also relax any white-knuckled passengers on your flight. They'll find music to be much more soothing than the sound of an aircraft engine, particularly while enroute between islands.

You may even want to select a route of flight that provides the proper scenery for the type of music you prefer. If you enjoy classical music, may I suggest a flight offshore Molokai's north shore or Kauai's Na Pali Coast. If your taste in music runs more to hard rock, a more appropriate flight would be over Hawaii's volcano area.

☐ Chevron credit card— As this book is written, all aviation fuel sold in Hawaii is distributed by the Chevron Oil Company. Consequently, their credit card is particularly useful. Some FBOs will give you a credit card to use on cross-country flights. Other FBOs will want you to take care of your own fuel purchases and the amount you spend on fuel will later be subtracted from your aircraft rental fee.

☐ Portable GPS— If you intend to fly cross-country and have access to a portable GPS, bring it. Many inter-island flights include moments when land is not visible in any direction. By using the GPS to confirm what the VOR indicates, you gain confidence that you are, indeed, proceeding as planned. CAUTION: Do not use GPS as your primary navigation means if you are somewhat unfamiliar with the technology. A light plane over the ocean is a poor place for making your learning mistakes.

FIGURING TRIP COSTS

The cost of an inter-island flight in a light plane is small when compared to the expense of an entire Hawaiian vacation, yet a light plane flight will likely be the most memorable experience of your visit to Hawaii.

Figure the cost of using a light plane in two parts: The cost of the checkout, and the cost of the flight itself. Plan on spending the equivalent of one hour of dual time if your checkout takes place at Honolulu International, and a somewhat shorter amount of time if done on a neighbor island. Some FBOs require short cross-country flights in their checkout process.

Flight time for trips will vary greatly, depending upon the route chosen. A flight around the island of Oahu will take about 1.5 hours, and a flight from Honolulu to the island of Hawaii, around that island, and then back to Honolulu will require over 5 hours.

TECHNIQUES TO BRUSH UP ON

Most visiting pilots could stand to brush up their skills in a couple of areas before beginning an inter-island touring flight. Because of the relatively strong winds that usually blow in Hawaii, the ability to use crosswind taxiing techniques is a must. Besides knowing where to place your controls while taxiing, you can also help avoid a tipover by remembering to taxi slowly. Most planes upset during taxi are those proceeding downwind at a higher than normal speed at the time a turn is attempted.

If time permits, you may also want to work on improving your abilities as a tour guide. Your audience may only consist of three passengers in a plane, but they'll certainly appreciate your efforts. Learn your material. Instead of just reading in this book about the sights you'll encounter during your flight, study the book. Memorize the names of volcanoes, waterfalls, and historical sites along your route. If you put enough time into your preparations, you can sound like an old-timer as you describe the sights.

Chapter 2
Island Weather

Good flying weather can usually be found in Hawaii throughout the year. Roughly one-quarter of all days are stormy enough to discourage aerial sightseeing, but if you are flexible in your schedule, you'll seldom be shut out from flying during your stay in Hawaii. Thunderstorms and other types of severe weather are infrequent, and blue sky is common. The prevailing winds are trade winds, which come from the Northeast. Winds from the opposite direction are called "Kona winds," and the weather associated with these is different enough from trade wind weather to deserve special attention in this chapter.

Hawaiian weather is mostly localized in nature. Large-scale weather such as fronts will occasionally swing over the Hawaiian Islands, but for the most part the weather found in Hawaii is generated by humid winds blowing against the local terrain. When wind hits a mountain, it must rise to climb over the terrain. The rising air cools, and, if it cannot hold all its moisture at the cooler temperature, clouds thicken and rain may fall. Meteorologists call this process orographic lifting. Rain falls on the windward sides of the islands, and when the wind remains a trade wind for several months at a time, the results can be striking. On the island of Molokai, for example, the cliffs on the northeastern (windward) side of the island may be covered in lush greenery while the terrain on the southwestern (leeward) side is so dry that cactus plants will grow. Sometimes rain showers formed on the windward sides of islands will drift slightly leeward of the mountains. On Oahu these showers are known as mauka showers (mountain showers).

Weather doesn't change greatly through the different seasons. Winter is perhaps 5 degrees cooler than summer, and rain showers are more common. Just as on the mainland, winter also brings more of the weather associated with fronts.

TRADE WIND CONDITIONS

Trade winds and their associated weather can be found in Hawaii most days of the year. Typically, Hawaii's trades will blow at about 15 knots with gusts to 20 or 25.

Before discussing the effects that trade winds have on flying conditions in Hawaii, we'll first examine the origin of these winds. Winds in general are created whenever atmospheric pressure varies between different points on the Earth. One cause of pressure differences is the uneven heating of the Earth's surface, and it is this process which drives the trade winds.

Over a year, the Earth's equator is hit at a more direct angle by the rays of the sun than any other area on the globe. Air above the equator heats to a temperature greater than that of the surrounding air, and it rises. This rising air then spreads out at high altitudes and leaves behind an area of low pressure. Once the air has risen, it travels north and south reaching latitudes of about 30 degrees, then descends. This descending air increases the pressure at these latitudes. Thus we find an area of high pressure at 30 degrees latitude and a band of low pressure over the equator.

Refer to Fig. 2-1. With high pressure over the 30 degree latitude and low pressure over the equator, wind is generated that moves from high pressure to low pressure. As the wind proceeds southward, it is bent to the right by coriolis force and heads southwest-

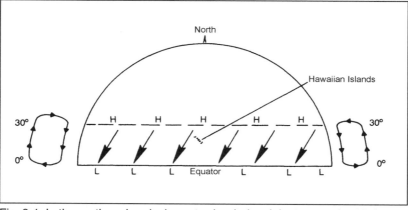

Fig. 2-1. In the northern hemisphere, trade winds originate near the 30 degree latitude and blow southwestward towards the equator.

8

ward. Thus the trade winds proceed from the Northeast to the Southwest. The latitude of the Hawaiian Islands varies between 22 degrees for Kauai and 19 degrees for the Big Island, putting Hawaii within the region of the trades. Notice that a trade wind is a relatively low-level wind. At altitudes above Hawaii where jets fly, the winds are usually from the west or southwest.

The model presented in Fig. 2-1 is, of course, a simplified view of the circulation of the Earth's atmosphere. Differences in heating of the Earth's surface develop not only because of latitude, but also due to differences between land heating and ocean heating. When a wind system created for reasons other than equatorial heating affects the islands, the normal trade wind flow may be altered. Nonetheless, the general circulation of trade winds prevails over the islands most of the time.

How do trade winds affect flying conditions in Hawaii? Crosswinds are not normally a problem. Public airports are built with at least one runway pointed toward the northeast. Kona's Ke-Ahole Airport is an exception to this rule, but it is so well shielded by nearby mountains that its surface winds are usually light when winds elsewhere are strong. At most airports, particularly Kahului Airport, care should be taken while taxiing to prevent winds from tipping the plane. Trade winds are strong enough to create enthusiastic turbulence in certain locations, and they're also strong enough to facilitate the orographic lifting of air that brings about rain showers.

Trade winds influence flying weather by creating atmospheric stability. The trades accomplish this by bringing cool air from the northeast to the lower levels of the Hawaiian atmosphere. Warmer temperatures can usually be found above the cool trade winds, and we end up with a temperature inversion. The altitude at which this inversion occurs varies from day to day but will usually be found between 5000 and 10,000 feet MSL. The inversion influences flying conditions in two ways: It acts as a ceiling to haze, and it prevents clouds from building up through it. On a typical day we'll find clouds that can be flown under at altitudes below 3000 feet or be flown over at altitudes above 6000 feet. A VFR pilot has his choice of flying the high road or the low road, and, with the exception of flights to Kauai, most light plane flying in Hawaii is done below the clouds.

Fig. 2-2. A view of the Hawaiian sky from 20,000 feet. (courtesy Jim Lockridge)

KONA WIND CONDITIONS

Sometimes the normal flow of trade winds will be replaced by Kona winds. A Kona wind is one from the southwest or anywhere near that direction. They're generally lighter in velocity than trade winds, although they'll occasionally really howl. When Kona winds are blowing, crosswinds are more likely than with trade winds, and forecasted surface winds should be compared closely with runway alignment at desired airports of use. Kona winds most frequently occur in winter.

The weather associated with Kona winds varies from trade wind weather. Kona winds are associated with some of the very best and worst weather to be found in the Hawaiian Islands. The change in wind direction changes the arrangement of temperatures at various altitudes, and this sets the stage for some unique weather (Fig. 2-2). Sometimes the sky will be nearly completely clear of clouds, a situation uncommon with trade winds. At other times huge cumulus buildups will form over the interior sections of islands and produce heavy rain. When winds are especially light, the air over the islands will heat up considerably more than the surrounding air and allow convective lifting instead of orographic lifting. This heating by the sun is most pronounced in afternoons, and on days with light Kona winds you can usually find the best flying weather during morning hours.

VISIBILITY

Pilots usually enjoy good visibility while flying in Hawaii. Smoke is seldom a problem, and Hawaii's sea level airports are hardly ever fogged in. Reductions in visibility are most often caused by rain showers or high levels of sea salt in the air. On a typical day, you can expect about 20 miles visibility below the haze layer and much greater visibility above that altitude.

Thanks to frequent winds and wide-open spaces, VFR flying is rarely prevented by smoke or smog. Pollution from urban areas is quickly removed by winds. Smoke from burning cane fields presents more of a potential problem, but it too is usually quickly dispersed. An unusually large source of smoke would be necessary to cause visibility in Hawaii to drop below VFR minimums, but such a source does exist: The volcanoes. When a volcano erupts on the island of Hawaii, keep an eye on the wind direction. Trade winds will blow most of the smoke away from the island chain, but Kona winds can bring enough smoke over the islands to create IFR conditions.

Rain showers present the most frequent threat to visual flying. Showers are an everyday occurrence in the islands, and a VFR pilot must either avoid the showers or determine that they can safely be flown through. One technique for staying out of rain on especially wet days is to fly on the leeward rather than windward sides of islands. For example, on a day with trade winds you will likely experience much drier conditions while enroute between Oahu and Maui if you fly south of Molokai instead of passing north of that island. Another technique for staying in the clear simply consists of waiting on the ground for acceptable flying conditions. Weather in Hawaii is usually of a localized nature, and if you don't like the weather you see, wait 20 minutes and then take another look.

Not all showers must be avoided, of course. Rain showers vary widely in size and intensity, and some do not seriously reduce visibility. The trick is to be able to tell the difference between the VFR showers and the IFR showers before entering them. When analyzing a rain storm, look at the vertical development of its clouds. Generally speaking, a cloud with substantial vertical development has the potential for producing heavier rainfall than a thin cloud. Also, try to look through a shower to the other side before entering it. Showers which can be seen through should not be a problem, but those which appear as a black wall should be avoided.

Keep in mind that you not only need to avoid spatial disorientation and collisions with terrain while in rain showers, you also have to stay clear of other air traffic. Rain showers can cause planes to be squeezed into using very similar altitudes. Keep a careful watch for other planes, turn on landing lights, and communicate with other potential traffic when visibility is reduced.

Ocean salt will reduce visibility when it is suspended in the air. Our atmosphere always has some salt floating in it, but there are days in Hawaii when the quantity of airborne salt is so great that visibility is reduced to 10 or 15 miles. Two variables determine how much sea salt is sent into the air: Wind velocity and size of ocean swells. As wind speed increases, the sea is tossed around more and more violently, whitecaps eventually form, and salt enters the air. Large ocean swells contribute to the air's salt content by creating heavy surf which breaks near the islands. When the surf is especially heavy, usually along the north shores of islands during winter, a pilot can see salt spray rising from the coastline as if it were a cloud of steam rising from boiling water.

Another visibility problem created by salt particles is the accumulation of these particles on aircraft windshields. After an hour or two of flight through heavily salt-laden air, a plane will pick up enough salt on its windshield to cause a drastic reduction in forward visibility. There's a simple solution to the problem: Wash the salt off with water. A bucketful of water thrown on a windshield will quickly and easily remove all salt. Sometimes, though, it may be impractical to land and throw some water on a plane's windshield. In such a case, find a small rain shower along your route and fly through it. Tell your passengers that a slight detour is necessary in order to wash the windows. When you emerge from the rain the salt will be gone, and you can then continue your flight without interruption.

FLYING IFR

Although Hawaiian weather usually permits flight between the islands in VFR conditions, there are those days when IFR is the only way to fly. A pilot must sacrifice sightseeing when flying by reference to instruments (the inside of Hawaiian clouds isn't very interesting), but he gains the ability to fly on days when the flight would otherwise not be possible. Conditions for IFR flying are nearly ideal: Icing is never a problem, thunderstorms are infrequent, and sea level airports are hardly ever obscured in fog. For someone who flies between the islands on a regular basis, an instrument rating is a valuable asset.

Not all instrument flying in Hawaii is done out of necessity, however. An IFR flight can be used to add an extra margin of safety to a trip which could also be flown in VFR conditions. Consider a flight from Oahu to Kauai, for example. There are days when cloud cover will keep VFR traffic below 3000 feet for the entire trip. At such altitudes, radar coverage and flight following are not possible, and engine malfunctions present a more serious threat. On the same days, IFR flights can often be conducted in blue sky at 6000 feet, and descents can be delayed until the destination island is reasonably close.

When planning an IFR flight in a single-engine plane, ask yourself, "If my engine should fail enroute and a ditching becomes necessary, will weather allow a search soon afterwards?" Your chances of rescue at sea diminish greatly with time, and if weather is solid IFR and not expected to improve within the next few hours, seriously consider delaying or cancelling your flight.

The localized nature of Hawaiian weather should be taken into account when choosing an alternate airport for your IFR flight. Even with favorable weather forecasts, airports will be hit by passing showers. Seldom does Hawaiian weather become lower than ILS minimums, but it will frequently drop below VOR approach minimums, particularly at the higher-altitude airports such as Molokai and Lanai. Consequently, you'd be wise to select an airport with an ILS as an alternate for your flight.

Here are two surprises you'll want to avoid. First, some fixed base operators will not rent planes when conditions are below VFR minimums. You may be a senior captain with United Airlines and still be denied the use of a plane. Inquire ahead of time about your FBO's policy towards IFR flights. Second, be aware that instrument approaches cannot be flown at night into some airports because approved weather-reporting is not available. Research the flight well before setting out.

SEVERE WEATHER

One of the most attractive aspects of flying in Hawaii is the rarity of severe weather. Thunderstorms develop in the islands only a few days each year. From time to time a waterspout will be spotted, and every few years the islands will be hit by a tropical storm or hurricane. Each of these types of severe weather can be enough to ruin your day if flown through but, fortunately, the vast majority of days in Hawaii are free of such weather.

Thunderstorms are infrequent in Hawaii primarily due to the usual stability of the atmosphere found in this part of the world. There's seldom a lack of moisture or lifting force to create small cumulus clouds, but once a growing cumulus reaches warmer air at the altitude of the trade wind inversion, it runs out of energy (latent heat of condensation) to grow higher. Occasionally a cumulus cloud building over the eastern end of the Big Island will have so much lifting force behind it that it will shoot through the inversion and find cooler air above in which to fully develop, but for the most part, trade wind days are free of thunderstorms. Fronts or certain types of Kona wind conditions are usually necessary before thunderstorms will form. When they do form, Hawaiian thunderstorms are often embedded within other clouds, and a plane should be radar-equipped to fly in such weather.

Waterspouts will sometimes be spotted in Hawaiian skies. They vary greatly in magnitude, ranging from small, dust-devil-like winds to enormous, tornado-like funnels. The smaller waterspouts may descend from small, fair weather cumulus clouds while the larger ones are always associated with cumulonimbus buildups. Waterspouts are formed when strong updrafts begin rotating due to atmospheric conditions such as wind shear. Unstable atmospheric conditions are necessary before waterspouts will form, thus they're more often found when Kona winds are blowing than during trade wind conditions. The shape of nearby terrain also influences the occurrence of waterspouts. The lightly sloping terrain of the Big Island must encourage the formation of waterspouts because more of these rotating winds are found off that island's Kona Coast than anywhere else in Hawaii. To avoid waterspouts, your best bet is to fly during daylight hours in order to pick them out visually.

The Hawaiian Islands are sometimes hit by storms that originate in the tropics. These tropical disturbances are cyclones hundreds of miles in diameter and are named according to their maximum wind speeds. A tropical depression is such a storm with winds of less than 33 knots, a tropical storm has maximum winds between 34 and 63 knots, and a hurricane has winds of 64 knots or greater. Generally speaking, the higher the wind speed, the greater will be the rainfall from such a storm. Most of us are accustomed to seeing weather moving from west to east, but tropical disturbances seldom travel in that direction. Their direction of movement can be unpredictable, and often it will be from east to west, followed by a swing towards the north. In November, 1982, the Hawaiian Islands were hit by Hurricane Iwa, Hawaii's first hurricane in 23 years. Its eye passed directly over the island of Niihau, and millions of dollars worth of damage was done on the islands of Kauai and Oahu. Ten years later, Hurricane Iniki pounded Kauai yet again. If a tropical storm or hurricane threatens the islands while you have a plane away from home base, communicate with your FBO to determine where and how the plane should be tied down.

TURBULENCE

The type of turbulence most commonly found in Hawaii is known as mechanical turbulence. It exists on the leeward side of islands whenever strong or moderate winds are blowing, and it is formed by wind hitting the jagged surfaces of the islands and then tumbling on the other side. The obvious way to avoid this turbulence is to fly on the windward sides of the islands. This means flying along north shores during trade wind conditions and along south shores when Kona winds are blowing.

A few notable exceptions to the typical model of mechanical turbulence exist in the islands. On the Big Island of Hawaii, for example, the mountains Mauna Kea and Mauna Loa provide such a wall against winds that you can fly along the Kona Coast when trade winds are blowing and fly in smooth air. However, at Kawaihae, the edge of the protected area, turbulence is usually very rough. On the island of Maui, McGregor Point at the south end of the central valley is known for its turbulence, and you should remain clear of this area when transitting the southern coast of Maui during times of strong trade winds. Lanai Airport also receives some unusual winds. When strong trades are blowing, they'll often curl like a breaking wave as they pass over the mountains northeast of the airport, and they'll then blow across Lanai Airport from the southwest! When such conditions exist, be prepared for wind shears during your approach.

PILOT WEATHER SERVICES

Pilots on all islands receive their weather briefings from the Honolulu Flight Service Station. There's no need to make a long distance call when on a neighbor island; toll-free telephone numbers are available (see Appendix B). A few of the services offered by the FSS are described below.

☐ Telephone Information Briefing Service (TIBS)— These are recorded messages which give a general forecast for specific routes or areas. When planning a flight, listen to TIBS before calling FSS for a personal briefing; FSS briefers like to pick up where TIBS left off. Pay attention to the forecasted visibility reductions in rain showers. Reductions to 5 miles are common, but forecasted reductions to 3 miles or less are a good clue that the day may be unsuitable for touring in a light plane.

☐ Terminal Forecasts (FT)— These airport weather forecasts are valid for 12 hour periods. They're updated daily at 8 a.m., 2 p.m., 8 p.m., and 2 a.m.

☐ Sequence Reports (SA)— These are the hourly weather reports for each airport. New reports become available approximately 5 minutes past each hour. Weather conditions in Hawaii change rapidly, and special reports during the hour (SP) are common.

Pilot Reports (PIREPS)— Pilot Reports are especially useful in Hawaii due to the localized and rapidly changing nature of the weather. You can pick these up either during your phone briefing or inflight.

Chapter 3
Cross-Country Flight Preparations

Preparing for a cross-country flight in Hawaii should be a two-part process. The first step consists of familiarizing yourself with those cross-country flying techniques that are used only in Hawaii. Hawaiian pilots have their own rule for determining cruising altitudes below 3000 feet, and Island Reporting Flight Plans are usually filed instead of regular VFR Flight Plans. Overwater navigation involves precautions not necessary for flight over land. This chapter is directed toward familiarizing you with these and other unique procedures.

The second step in flight planning consists of making the type of calculations you would for a flight anywhere in the country, but making them with extreme care. Fuel computations should include a generous reserve because fuel is unavailable on some islands and because your flight will be overwater. Heading and time enroute calculations may be greatly affected by the typically strong trade winds. Of course your preparations should also include a detailed weather briefing.

ISLAND REPORTING FLIGHT PLANS

Although standard VFR Flight Plans may be used for inter-island flights, you are advised to instead file an "island reporting flight plan." Under the island reporting service, you make position reports to FSS when over designated checkpoints along your route (Fig. 3-1). The flight service station keeps track of your progress and will inform you of NOTAMs or significant weather changes. If one of your reports is 15 minutes overdue and FSS cannot establish communications with you, preparations for search and rescue operations will begin.

17

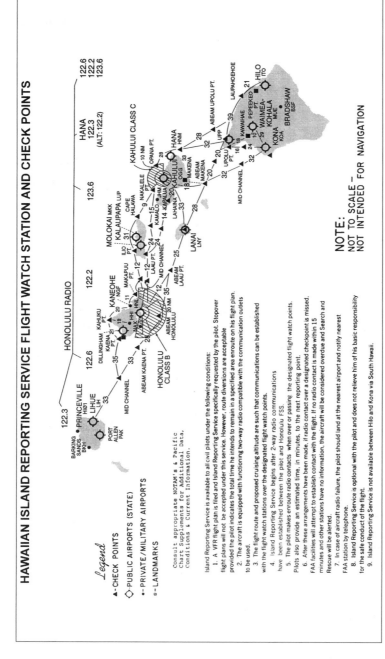

Fig. 3-1. Hawaiian Island reporting service flight watch check points. (courtesy FAA)

18

Fig. 3-2. In Hawaii light planes are real workhorses. Pilot Paul Wessel is shown unloading cargo on the island of Lanai.

To obtain island reporting service, describe your type of flight plan as "VFR island reporting" instead of "VFR" when filing. The remainder of the flight plan is filed in the same manner as standard VFR flight plans. Once aloft, give FSS a call to activate the flight plan and inform them of your off time. FSS will then let you know which checkpoint to report next. Touch-and-go landings may be performed at enroute airports if flight service is aware of your plans. However, an island reporting flight plan must be closed prior to any full-stop landings. If the airport you'll be landing at has approach control or a tower control, close your flight plan prior to contacting the controller.

There are a few disadvantages to using island reporting service. First, pilots enroute to Kauai often find that when the service is used along with traffic advisories from Honolulu Center, the necessary switching between frequencies can become distracting. Kauai-bound pilots flying at altitudes too low for Center advisories should definitely file island reporting flight plans, but those who fly at higher altitudes may instead choose the combination of straight VFR flight plans and flight following from Center. Second, if radio failure prevents you from making a position report on time, you'll need to land at a nearby airport in order to quickly telephone flight service and prevent an unnecessary search from being organized.

The advantages of using island reporting services are obvious. Your chances of being rescued after a ditching are best if search and rescue operations are begun soon after the ditching and searchers

19

have a good idea of where to look. Island reporting flight plans are superior to straight VFR flight plans in these respects.

CRUISING ALTITUDES AT OR BELOW 3000 FEET

The majority of light plane flying in Hawaii takes place at altitudes of 3000 feet and below. Federal aviation regulations do not designate cruising altitudes for planes flying this low, so instead the pilots of Hawaii have agreed upon their own rule to govern Cruising altitudes at or below 3000 feet MSL. The rule is as follows:

Westbound flights— 1000, 2000, or 3000 feet MSL
Eastbound flights— 500, 1500, or 2500 feet MSL

This cruising rule is observed by virtually all light planes flying in Hawaii (Fig. 3-2). There is an easy way to remember the cruising altitude rule. The lowest VFR cruising altitude by the FAA's rules is 3500 feet for eastbound flights. Work backwards in 500 foot increments from this altitude while alternating direction of flight and you'll have Hawaii's rule (3000 feet westbound, 2500 feet eastbound, 2000 feet westbound, etc.).

NORTH SHORES VS. SOUTH SHORES

Should your route of flight proceed north or south of enroute islands? When making your decision, consider these three factors: scenery, rain showers, and turbulence. On the point of scenery, a flight along the north shores wins the contest easily. Trade winds bring much more rain to the northern sides of islands, and the rains are necessary for sustaining lush, tropical greenery. However, north shore showers can become a problem on days when especially moist air is brought in by the trade winds. On such days a flight along the southern shores of islands will give you the best chance of continuing your flight while remaining VFR. Turbulence can be avoided by flying on whichever side of the islands the wind is coming from. When all three factors are considered, your best bet for a touring flight on a typical trade wind day would be to fly your first leg along the north shores to take advantage of the smooth air and fine scenery. If rain showers prevent your trip along the north shore of an island, continue your trip along the south shore of that island and try to view its northern shore on your return trip.

RECOMMENDED TIME OF DAY FOR FLIGHTS

Some hours of the day are better than others for inter-island flights. On days when light Kona winds are forecast, the mornings

Fig. 3-3. A Pitts enroute between islands (courtesy Jim Lockridge)

usually provide better flying weather than afternoons. However, on days with trade wind conditions, you will often find fewer showers enroute if you avoid an early morning flight and fly instead during the middle of the day.

Weather is not the only factor to be considered. Whenever you fly a single-engine plane between islands, keep in mind that there is always a slight chance the engine will fail and a ditching will become necessary. You should allow yourself at least one hour to be spotted in the water and another hour to be rescued. Thus, it makes a great amount of sense to arrive at your destination at least two hours before sunset. Search and rescue operations can seldom be successfully conducted in the dark, and you and your raft could drift great distances before sunrise of the next day.

OVERWATER NAVIGATION

Chances are that your first cross-country flight in Hawaii will also be your first extended overwater flight. Overwater flying is more demanding than flying over land due to the lack of enroute landmarks, but if you plan your flight carefully and take advantage of the state's VOR facilities, the navigating should still be relatively easy.

To reduce the possibility of major errors, take a few steps to ensure that your navigational instruments are giving you accurate information. Conduct a VOR check while in the runup area. At Honolulu International, you can use the VOR test frequency of 111.0 MHz, and at other airports use ground checkpoints. Of course your VOR must be tuned to the correct frequency to give accurate information inflight, and the best way to double-check the frequency is to listen to the station identifier. Check your compass against runway heading when in position and holding. Yes, even your faithful friend the compass can lie. Sometimes a radio will become magnetized and pull the compass 30 degrees or more away from an accurate reading. Excessive compass deviations can also be caused by metal objects placed near the compass. Finally, compare the reading of your heading indicator to that of your compass frequently throughout the flight.

While enroute between islands, and particularly when heading toward Kauai, beware of "phantom Islands." A group of clouds and their shadows below can sometimes look amazingly like an island when seen from a distance, and if you change your course and pursue one of these phantom islands you'll have about as much chance of finding land as a thirsty desert traveler would have catching a mirage. Instead, continue on your planned heading and use the VOR to confirm that you're flying in the right direction. If your estimated time of arrival comes up and the island still isn't in sight, or if your VOR indicator shows indications that you're not expecting, it's time to seek help.

LOST PROCEDURES

If you become lost during a cross-country flight in Hawaii, use your radio to quickly obtain assistance from radar controllers. One of the biggest complaints voiced by controllers who have worked such emergencies is that often a pilot will wait until his fuel is low before calling for assistance. The controller can usually identify the plane and give vectors to the nearest airport, but if the plane runs out of fuel enroute, it's going to have to ditch anyway. When calling for assistance, you may choose to use the appropriate frequency for Honolulu Center (see Appendix) or emergency frequency 121.5. A transponder squawk of 7700 will help to alert ground personnel of your troubles.

ENROUTE TRAFFIC AVOIDANCE

Make a special effort to watch for other traffic during your tour of the islands. Most light planes in Hawaii fly the same routes between airports (staying just offshore) and fly at only a few different altitudes (between 1500 and 3000 feet MSL). Consequently, a large percentage of the state's air traffic is concentrated within a relatively small piece of the sky. Watching closely for other traffic and flying at appropriate altitudes are your two best actions for avoiding a close encounter with another airplane. However, you can also help yourself avoid other traffic by using plane-to-plane communications and scheduling your trip so as to miss the flights of scheduled tour planes.

In Hawaii, professional air tour planes traverse the skies daily. Several different companies are based in Honolulu and fly tourists among the islands in light twins. Sometimes several of these planes will travel in a pack spread out over a few miles, and traffic avoidance can become very interesting if you should fly into one of these packs. The tour planes typically follow the same schedule. Departures from Honolulu take place at about 8 a.m. with flights proceeding over Lanai to either Maui or the Big Island for lunch stops. Then in early afternoon they're airborne again and heading along the north shore of Molokai and over Oahu enroute to Kauai. Kauai is circled in a clockwise direction, and the planes then land at Lihue Airport for a few hours to allow the passengers to take a boat trip. In late afternoon the tour planes depart Lihue and race to Honolulu International like horses heading to the barn at the end of the day.

Plane-to-plane communications on frequency 122.9 are heavily used in Hawaii. A typical transmission will be structured such as: "North Shore Molokai Traffic, Cessna 761HB is approaching Ilio Point at 2500, eastbound." Although most transmissions are made by commuter airline pilots, all pilots are encouraged to participate. The north and south shores of Molokai are heavily traveled routes and generate a great number of plane-to-plane communications. Pilots flying along Maui's shoreline between Opana Point and the eastern corner of the island should address transmissions to "Hana Traffic," and for flights along the northern shore of the Big Island, transmissions should be addressed to "Hamakua Coast Traffic."

Chapter 4
Safety Procedures

Single-engine cross-country flying in Hawaii can be safer than you'd imagine. The factors with the greatest bearing upon the safety of a flight are those which are most within your control: The decision to fly in existing weather or wait for an improvement, the decision of how close to fly to hazardous terrain, and other such choices. Just as on the mainland, engine failures are not the principal safety hazard for cross-country flights. Certainly, no one enjoys the thought of experiencing an engine failure over the open ocean. However, modern aircraft engines have a high level of dependability, and even when they do fail (usually from a lack of fuel), the record of ditchings in Hawaii show that the plane's occupants stand a good chance of surviving the impact and being picked up quickly thereafter. The success of the ditching and subsequent rescue depends in large part upon the pilot's knowledge of ditching procedures and upon the preparations that had been made for the ditching.

EQUIPMENT

What equipment should a plane contain on a Hawaiian cross-country that wouldn't be needed on a mainland cross-country? First, let's look at the regulations. FAR 91.205 requires that an aircraft operated for hire over water and beyond power-off gliding distance from shore be equipped with approved flotation gear readily available to each occupant and at least one pyrotechnic signaling device. You'll nearly always find these items aboard rental planes. There are other FARs concerning overwater flying, but they do not apply to personal travel in light planes. Described below are

25

pieces of equipment, both required and non-required, which can add safety to an overwater flight.

Life Vests

One of your most important preflight activities should be checking to see that every occupant of your plane has a suitable life vest and knows how to use it. You can expect to find inflatable airline-type vests in all rental planes. Putting the vests on before takeoff is an excellent idea, and some flying schools in Hawaii require this practice from their students. You only have to watch a few groups of passengers trying to put on their vests while standing on an uncrowded parking ramp to realize that, in an emergency, many of them would be unable to correctly put on their vests before splashdown. Certainly you'll want all children on your flight to wear their vests. Just about the only suitable alternative to wearing a vest during the flight is to wear a life vest-containing belt (Fig. 4-1) and to have had practice putting on the vest, both on the ground and in the water.

Fig. 4-1. Flight instructor Amy Stevens Hughes wears a life-vest belt .

Rafts

As strange as it might seem, there are rental planes in Hawaii that do not come equipped with life rafts. Even if the plane you checked out in had a raft, you can't depend on finding a raft in the plane you'll be taking on your trip. Ask the operator of your FBO about the availability of a raft for the particular plane you'll be flying.

We renters can greatly influence whether those rental planes currently without rafts will be equipped with rafts in the future. When you call an FBO to discuss the rental of a plane, specifically ask if the plane is equipped with a raft. If it isn't and you'd prefer to fly in a raft-equipped plane, take your business elsewhere. Rafts are expensive (costing between $400 and $600) and the managers of several FBOs will need to realize that they're losing business before they'll purchase rafts. Appendix B of this book describes the availability of rafts at each major FBO in Hawaii. Those FBOs described as not offering rafts in all their planes may have added rafts by the time you are ready to rent a plane, and a telephone call should be used to determine the current status of raft availability.

You'll definitely want to have a raft on board for a flight to Kauai because a ditching in the channel between Oahu and Kauai could mean a longer-than-normal amount of time in the water before help arrives. If your plane should sink before rescuers arrive, you'd be nearly impossible to spot without a raft.

ELTs

A functioning emergency locator transmitter can be a great aid to searchers for locating an airplane that has ditched. ELTs will be found in all rental planes, but nine times out of ten, these units are permanently installed. Consequently, when the plane sinks, so does the ELT. The type of ELT that can be removed and carried into a life raft would be ideal for Hawaiian light planes, but you won't see many of these. If you fly regularly between the islands, seriously consider purchasing a personal ELT.

Pyrotechnic Signaling Devices

These are flares and other types of sophisticated fireworks used by downed pilots for catching the attention of passing ships and planes. Pyrotechnic signaling devices should be treated with a great amount of respect. If a flare is ignited inside the cabin of an airborne plane, the pilot may become incapable of controlling the flight within a matter of seconds due to fire and smoke.

In 1979, a flight instructor and student practicing touch-and-goes at Ford Island Airport in a Cessna 152 discovered the consequences of setting off a flare inside a plane. Someone had left a loaded and cocked pencil flare inside the plane's glove compartment, and when the instructor closed the door to the compartment after it came open, the flare ignited and shot across the cabin. It lodged in the ceiling near fuel lines and immediately filled the cabin with smoke. The plane was just a few hundred feet high when the flare went off, and the instructor chose to turn around and attempt a downwind landing. Smoke became so thick that the instructor couldn't see, but when he opened a side window to let some of the smoke out, the cabin filled with fire. He closed the window and was able to see just well enough to land the plane. The instructor opened the plane's left door and pushed the student out even before the plane had stopped rolling, and then jumped out himself. Within 10 seconds after the plane stopped rolling, its wings collapsed from the fire. Fortunately, both occupants of the plane survived this ordeal.

Two precautions will ensure that one of these devices is not accidentally triggered in your plane. During your preflight inspection, check that your signaling devices are properly packaged. Then don't allow anyone to fool with them in flight. It's that simple.

If you ever find yourself in a life raft and in need of igniting one of these items, be careful. Hold the flare a good distance away from your eyes and downwind when you ignite it.

DITCHING

This is a section which, hopefully, you'll read well but never have to use. Pilots who learn to fly in Hawaii usually do a pretty good job of mentally preparing themselves for the possibility of one day having to ditch. A private pilot who learned to fly in Hawaii once jokingly told me the story of his first mainland flight. He said that after flying over hundreds of miles of barren desert terrain he was suddenly frightened by the realization that if the engine should quit, where could he ditch? If you're mentally prepared for the possibility of a ditching, you'll do a better job at it.

One secret to this mental preparation is organization. Here are the major components to pre-ditching preparation: (1) Turn towards land and attempt an engine restart; (2) Communicate your situation; and (3) Prepare the airplane. Touchdown techniques and after-the-ditching procedures will also be discussed.

Turn Towards Land and Attempt An Engine Restart

As in any engine failure situation, your first steps are to maintain flying speed and find a place to land. Since the ocean offers an infinite number of places to put a plane down, you'll probably want to just turn towards land and concentrate on other details until you reach a lower altitude.

Even if you can't reach land, ditching close to land has advantages over an open ocean ditching. First, you may find water which is smoother than the open ocean, particularly if you're heading for the leeward side of an island. Second, your rescue after the ditching should be easier.

Once you are pointed in the right direction, you'll want to attempt a restart. Memorize a panel scan which will allow a quick troubleshooting of all common problems. A popular method is to start at the fuel selector valve; move up to the mixture, throttle and carb heat; and then move horizontally toward the ignition. If your restart attempts are unsuccessful, you'll quickly want to proceed with other preparations.

Communicate

Pre-ditching communications are vital. The sooner rescuers start looking for you, and the more accurate idea they have of where to look, the better the chance is that they'll find you.

First, let's look at which frequency to use. If you're already talking to a controller who has radar (such as an approach or departure controller), then stay on that frequency. Otherwise, use emergency frequency 121.5. When you speak on 121.5, just about every ground station within reception range will be alerted by the call.

Now, here's what to say. Start your call with something that will catch the attention of the controllers. "Mayday! Mayday!" will do the trick. Immediately follow this with who you are (Cessna 4321B), where you are (six miles south of Molokai's Lau Point), and what is wrong (engine failure, will be ditching). You should soon hear a response to your broadcast, and you may be asked a question or two. How much time you spend conversing with individuals on the ground should depend upon your altitude remaining and whether your initial transmission was understood. Also, unless asked otherwise, set emergency code 7700 on your transponder.

Prepare the Airplane

Several preparations should be made before touchdown. These actions will reduce the possibility of injury during the deceleration and shorten the amount of time necessary for leaving the airplane.

☐ Secure or jettison any heavy objects. Unlatch the doors of the plane and slip an empty shoe between each door and the fuselage to hold the door open a crack. If the ditching is not a smooth one, the fuselage could bend a bit and make opening an unprepared door extremely difficult.

☐ Instruct everyone who isn't already wearing a life vest to put their vests on. Do not inflate the vests until outside the plane.

☐ Ensure that seatbelts and shoulder harnesses are on and snug. Those backseat passengers without shoulder harnesses should lean forward and assume the emergency landing position.

☐ If time permits, distribute the safety equipment. Put one passenger in charge of the raft, one in charge of the signaling devices, and another in charge of the portable ELT. When the time comes to leave the plane, confusion will be reduced.

Touchdown Technique

A successful ditching involves many of the same techniques required for a successful emergency landing on solid ground. Both wind direction and surface conditions should be taken into account when choosing a direction of flight for touchdown, and the touchdown should be made under control and at the slowest possible speed. An ideal ditching would involve a touchdown while the plane is pointed into the wind and flying parallel to any ocean swells. Conditions don't usually allow such a textbook ditching, however, and some type of compromise is often necessary.

Determining wind direction is usually a simple matter. If moderate or strong trade winds were blowing at your airport of departure, chances are that the winds will be from the northeast throughout most of the island chain. Look for windstreaks and other indications of wind direction upon the ocean's surface.

Determining sea conditions is a more complex matter. The sea will likely be disturbed by both waves and swells. Swells can best be spotted in the early morning or late afternoon when the sun is near the horizon. Although they may be difficult to spot under certain conditions, swells will create valleys and ridges on the ocean surface which can measure eight feet or more from top to bottom and seriously affect the outcome of a ditching. If a touchdown must be made perpendicular to the swells, a touchdown on the backside rather than the approaching face of a swell is best. Waves are surface disturbances caused by the local winds. When wind speed exceeds 15 knots or so, waves will break and cause whitecaps. Although they're usually more visible than swells, waves do not present as much of a threat to ditching planes as swells do, and care should be taken to prevent confusing waves and swells.

After wind and sea conditions have been examined, you'll need to make your decision as to which direction of flight to use for touchdown. If wind speed is 20 knots or greater, a touchdown into the wind will likely produce satisfactory results. A plane slowed down to 45 knots and flying into a 20 knot headwind will have a very survivable groundspeed for touchdown. When winds are lighter than 20 knots, you'll need to use your judgment and compare the windspeed to swell heights when making your touchdown heading decision.

The touchdown should take place at the slowest possible speed. However, a safe glide speed should be maintained until just a few feet above the water's surface in order to prevent a touchdown with a high sink rate. Water has about as much cushioning effect as concrete when contacted at landing speed, and a high sink rate at touchdown will likely result in injuries to occupants of the plane. One of the best ways to ditch with both a slow speed and only a slight descent rate is to use power, if available, during the ditching. If fuel is nearly gone and there is no chance of reaching land, a ditching while power is still available may be a wise course of action.

UNTIL HELP ARRIVES

Once your plane comes to a stop, it's time to get out quickly. If water has risen above the level of the door, the plane's cabin may need to take on some water before a door can be fully opened. That shoe which you earlier stuck between the door and the fuselage will help bring about this process of pressure equalization.

Upon exiting the plane, life vests and the raft may be inflated. Care should be taken to keep a hand on a raft while it is inflating. As Frank Kingston Smith points out in *Private Pilot's Survival Manual*, "An unsecured raft is very likely to blow away in any kind of breeze, and once out of reach, no one in the water encumbered with clothing and an inflated life vest can catch up to it."

Make every effort to stay next to the airplane as long as it is floating. The plane will be considerably easier to spot than the raft, and the plane's ELT may also help rescuers find you.

If ground personnel had been alerted by radio about your ditching, you stand a good chance of being spotted and rescued within two hours. While waiting for rescuers to arrive, keep as much of your skin as possible covered with clothing. The sunburn and dehydration that can result from skin exposed to sunlight may seriously affect your health if rescue is delayed. Keep your morale high by picturing how beautiful the sight of an approaching helicopter or boat will be.

STATISTICS

Just how often do ditchings occur in Hawaii and what are the outcomes? According to information released by the National Transportation Safety Board, eleven ditchings involving single-engine planes occurred in Hawaiian waters during the ten-year period of 1/1/70 through 12/31/79. In nine of these accidents, all occupants escaped without serious injuries. Both of the other two accidents involved the eventual rescue of one front-seat occupant and the loss of lives of the other occupants. Two ditchings took place after dark, and one of these involved fatalities.

Although the numbers to consider here are small, a few preliminary conclusions can be reached. First, the survival of at least one occupant in each ditching indicates that the deceleration during a controlled ditching in Hawaiian waters is normally survivable. The evacuation from the plane and the wait until help arrives are the times when life is most often lost. Second, daytime ditchings are more likely to be successful than nighttime ditchings. When all factors are considered, the odds that the occupants of a light plane will survive a ditching are good provided that the ditching takes place in daylight, steps are taken to ensure a quick evacuation, and enough survival equipment is removed from the plane to keep the occupants from drowning until help arrives.

During the 1990s, ten additional ditchings occurred in Hawaiian waters (although many of these were in open ocean, related to ferry flights). All occupants escaped with no injuries or just minor injuries in eight of ten ditchings. These statistics reinforce the lessons of the 1980s.

FORCED LANDINGS

Not all engine failures in Hawaii occur over water, of course. The selection of suitable terrain for a forced landing can be difficult for a pilot accustomed to flying over the mainland, and so a few pointers are given here. First, save yourself the trouble of looking for a newly cut wheat field, you'd have to glide more than 2000 miles to find one. Most Hawaiian agricultural lands consist of sugar cane fields, and these may be used for emergency landings when no better terrain can be found. Pick a yellow field, which is a tall and mature field, because it will provide the most cushioning. Your airplane will likely be damaged during the landing, but you should be able to walk away from it. Watch out for irrigation ditches. Also, most of the roads cut through the cane fields are too narrow to land on without putting your wings in the cane, but if you touch down reasonably near a road you'll have only a short hike through the cane to reach it.

More forced landings have probably been made on golf courses than any other type of solid terrain in Hawaii. Remember to consider the wind direction and velocity when choosing a fairway.

Some types of terrain should be avoided. Beaches are usually too crowded to be safely landed upon, and lava rock is usually too rough. There are many locations through the islands where a ditching slightly offshore would be safer than landing on the available terrain.

TERRAIN AVOIDANCE

There's something overwhelming about flying in Hawaii. The adventurer in each of us is brought out when we fly in a land where waterfalls plummet thousands of feet to the sea; where high-walled valleys, lined with lush tropical greenery, stretch back into the hearts of the islands; and where those giants of the ocean, the whales, break the surface of the sea with their spouting geysers and powerful tails. We can easily imagine ourselves to be young Lindberghs or heroic explorers. Yet, herein lies a problem. A boldness often accompanies our elation, and we can be inspired to venture closer to the terrain than we would in less exotic surroundings. The purpose of this section is not to discourage that great feeling which flying in Hawaii can produce. Rather, it is to acquaint you with those types of terrain flying which should be avoided.

The most important advice that you can receive about avoiding hazardous terrain in Hawaii is this: Don't fly up those inviting valleys which open to the sea. The mouth of a valley may be wide enough to turn a plane around in, but as you fly further inland, you may not notice soon enough that the valley is becoming narrower. Furthermore, as the valley reaches inland it will usually angle uphill. Winds in the valley may be quite turbulent, and with all these factors working against you, you may not be able to fly the plane out of the valley.

In recent years Hawaiian valleys have trapped both high-time pilots and novices. Most visiting pilots have the good sense to avoid valley flying. However, if you are intent on examining a valley from your plane, at least choose a day without clouds and wind, and ensure that your flight starts at the top of a valley and then proceeds downhill towards the sea.

You'll want to avoid certain types of high-altitude sightseeing. Many pilots are surprised to learn that both Maui and Hawaii include mountains which tower more than 10,000 feet above sea level. In order to view the scenic peaks of these volcanic mountains safely from a nearby light plane, a few precautions are necessary, primarily due to the poor climb performance which non-turbocharged planes show at high altitudes.

Begin by checking the winds aloft forecasts at 9,000 and 12,000 feet for the island you'll be visiting. If wind speeds are forecasted to be 30 knots or greater, choose another day for your high-altitude sightseeing. Strong winds will create moderate to severe turbulence that can extend miles downwind from the mountains. Downdrafts on the lee side of the mountains are also created by strong winds, and the downdrafts can easily exceed the climb performance of most light planes at these altitudes.

Another precaution to observe in high-altitude flying is to always leave yourself an easy route to lower altitude. Strong turbulence and downdrafts can be encountered with little warning near high mountains, and you'll want to be able to turn your plane towards lower terrain with a heading change of no more than 45 degrees. For this reason, flights in non-turbocharged aircraft are not recommended through the saddle between Hawaii's two highest mountains, Mauna Kea and Mauna Loa.

Finally, keep in mind that the biggest cause of fatal accidents in Hawaii during the 1990s was collisions with rising terrain during night or low visibility operations. Hawaii is a mountainous state with abrupt terrain features. Avoid flying through rain showers you can't see through, and treat night flight operations with a high degree of seriousness.

Chapter 5
Flying From Honolulu International and Kalaeloa

Honolulu International is an airport which should be studied carefully before being used (Fig. 5-1). It is one of our country's fifteen busiest airports, a large percentage of its traffic consists of jumbo jets, and it is surrounded by Class B Airspace. If you wish to fly from Honolulu but lack experience operating from such a major airport, first brush up your knowledge of wake turbulence avoidance and Class B procedures. All visiting pilots, regardless of experience, will need to acquaint themselves with those procedures peculiar to Honolulu International Airport. The terrain around Honolulu International, the existence of other nearby airports, and the need to expedite traffic have required that very specific arrival and departure routes be established. You must be familiar with these routes and other unique procedures covered in this chapter before you can fit smoothly into the flow of traffic.

A checkout from Honolulu International will most likely involve touch and go landings at Kalaeloa Airport. Since the arrival and departure flows of traffic at Kalaeloa are unique, special attention to that airport is given at the end of this chapter.

The majority of light planes in Hawaii are based at Honolulu International, and chances are that your first inter-island flight will originate there. To give you an idea of what to expect during a checkout flight, a sample checkout flight is described.

For an overview of Honolulu International, take a look at Fig. 5-2. You'll notice that the runways are connected by a great number of taxiways, and you are advised to carry an airport diagram with you whenever you fly from this airport.

Fig. 5-1. Honolulu International Airport (courtesy Dan Savino).

Controllers will sometimes use names not listed on a diagram to describe areas on the airport. Runway 8R-26L is sometimes referred to as the "Reef Runway" (NASA has designated the Reef Runway as an alternate landing site for the space shuttle). Also, the parking areas for general aviation aircraft are grouped together into two categories. The "North Ramp" is the area northwest of Runway 4L-22R but east of the airport's main terminal, and the "South Ramp" is the area southeast of Runway 4R-22L.

CLASS B AIRSPACE

Honolulu International Airport is surrounded by Class B Airspace (Fig. 5-3). As a pilot, you must ensure that your plane is equipped with suitable two-way radio, and altitude-encoding transponder. If you are returning to Honolulu and your VOR or transponder fails, inform ATC as soon as possible about the failure. If the failure involves your radio and you haven't yet contacted Honolulu Approach, plan to land at an airport other than Honolulu International. You might choose Molokai Airport if approaching from the east or Dillingham if approaching from the west. From such an airport you can give Honolulu Tower a call on the telephone to make arrangements for your arrival. Honolulu International definitely isn't the type of airport you'd want to arrive at unexpected and without a radio.

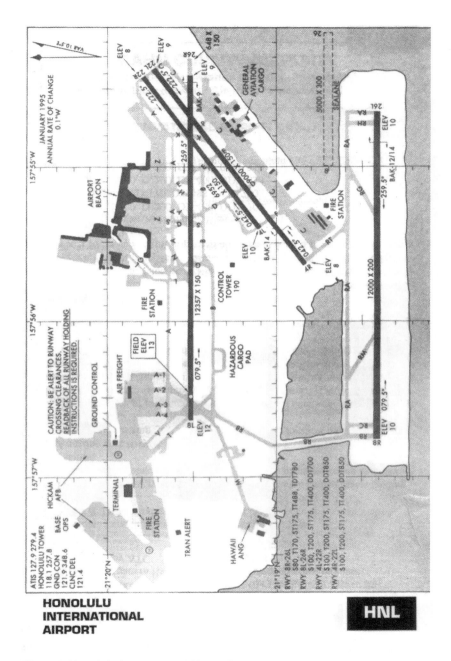

Fig. 5-2. Honolulu International Airport Diagram.

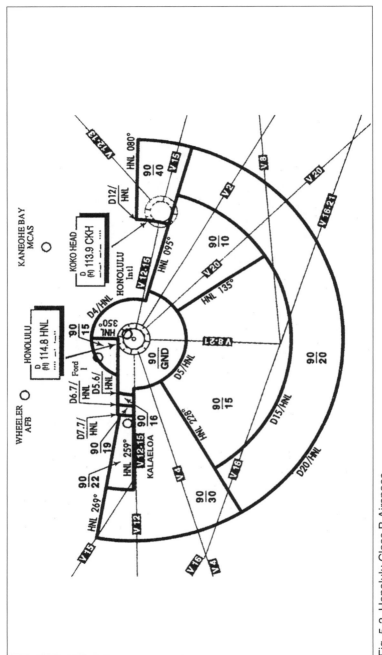

Fig. 5-3. Honolulu Class B Airspace.

Your other duty concerning Class B Airspace is to receive a clearance before entering. While approaching Oahu on a cross-country flight, keep in mind that approach control frequencies are often congested, and it would be in your best interest to receive clearance well before reaching the airspace boundary.

AIRPORT PROCEDURES

A few of the procedures used at Honolulu International Airport may vary from those used at airports you're more familiar with. Described below are three procedures you should be aware of.

Simultaneous Runway Operations— During daylight hours when runways are dry, the tower may put all four runways to use at one time. Light planes may be departing on Runways 4, a Boeing 737 may be landing on Runway 8L, and a flight of military aircraft may be departing Runway 8R, all simultaneously. The tower accomplishes this feat of apparent magic by requiring landing aircraft to hold short of intersecting runways. While this system allows greater utilization of runways, it also has a few disadvantages. Imagine an instance in which you have been cleared to land on Runway 4L but told to hold short of Runway 8L. A jet begins its takeoff roll on Runway 8L and immediately afterwards you determine that you must make a go-around (for whatever reason). You obviously do not wish to reach the intersection of the two runways at the same time and altitude as the jet, and some quick action and communicating may be required.

A more likely conflict between airplanes using intersecting runways could occur when one of the pilots misunderstands a communication and begins his takeoff at the same time a plane on the other runway is rolling for takeoff. In both of the instances mentioned here the moral of the story is the same: Be aware of what is happening on a runway which intersects your runway.

Runup Before Taxiing Out—Engine runups and before takeoff checklists should be conducted in the designated runup areas near the FBOs. Controllers expect you to be ready for takeoff by the time you finish taxiing to the runway.

Contacting Tower When Ready for Takeoff—At many airports, the tower will clear planes for takeoff in the order in which they have called ready for takeoff. This is not the case at Honolulu International. Honolulu controllers wish to discourage unnecessary transmissions, and if you are the third plane in line at a particular runway intersection, you will be the third plane to be cleared for takeoff from there. Only when you are number one should you call the tower.

VFR APPROACH AND DEPARTURE ROUTES

In order to better control the flow of traffic in the vicinity of Honolulu International Airport, ATC has established specific approach and departure routes for VFR aircraft. You should be very familiar with these routes before operating from the airport. As you read the following descriptions of routes, try to trace the routes on the enlarged chart of Oahu which appears on the back of a Hawaiian Island Sectional Aeronautical Chart. Some of the names of highways or other points along the routes may be unfamiliar to you. If this is the case, ask the flight instructor who handles your checkout flight to point out the various routes during the flight. Every few years the procedures for arriving at and departing Honolulu International are amended. Check with your FBO to make sure that the procedures described below are current.

DEPARTURES—The departure procedure you choose will depend upon your desired direction of flight and the runways in use. Contact Clearance Delivery (121.4) prior to taxi, stating requested departure route.

Tradewind Procedures (Runways 4&8)

Shoreline Four departure*— Runways 4 maintain runway heading to H-1 freeway, Runway 8L maintain runway heading to Nimitz Highway, thence right direct to the center of Honolulu Harbor. Fly one mile offshore, abeam Kewalo basin, then direct one mile south of Diamond Head. Turn left and remain within two miles of the shoreline until out of Class B airspace. Maintain 1,500' MSL in Class B Airspace.

Freeway Four departure— Runways 4 maintain runway heading to H-1 freeway, Runway 8L turn left to parallel Runways 4 to H-1 freeway, thence right turn, resume own navigation via H-1 freeway eastbound, then via the Kalanianaole Highway until passing abeam Koko Head. Maintain 1,500' MSL in Class B airspace. Intended for single-engine aircraft and usable only during daylight.

Red Hill Three departure— Runways 4 maintain runway heading to Moanalua Road; Runway 8L turn left to parallel Runways 4 to Moanalua road, then left over Moanalua Road, northwest until out of Class B airspace. Maintain 1,500' MSL in Class B airspace. Caution for VFR traffic inbound to H-1/H-2 interchange descending through 1,500' MSL.

NOTE: Shoreline Four normally limited to twin-engine aircraft.

Kona Wind Procedures

Kona Three departure— Turn left heading 180 degrees for radar vectors eastbound. Expect vectoring 5 or more miles south of Diamond Head to avoid the 26L LDA final approach course. Maintain 1500' MSL in the Class B airspace.

West Loch Three departure— Turn right as soon as practical until north of Runway 26R, thence direct to center of West Loch, Pearl Harbor. Maintain 1,500' while in Class B airspace. CAUTION: VFR traffic eastbound to the H-1/H-2 Interchange descending to or below 2,000' MSL.

ARRIVALS— Contact approach control and receive clearance before entering Class B and Class D airspace. HNL Class B airspace is established from the HNL VORTAC. High density traffic in the vicinity of the H-1/H-2 interchange.

North arrival— Contact approach control prior to the H-1/H-2 interchange. Expect clearance via H-1/H-2 interchange direct Navy/Marine Golf Course. Enter left downwind Runways 4/8L or right downwind Runways 22/26R as assigned. Frequency 119.1.

West arrival— Contact approach control prior to Kahe Power Plant. Expect clearance via the Kahe Power Plant direct H-1/H-2 interchange direct Navy/Marine Golf Course. Enter downwind as assigned. Frequency 119.1.

East arrival Runways 4/8L— Contact approach control prior to NORBY intersection (MKK 262 radial 20 DME and CKH 112 radial 12 DME). Expect clearance via MKK 262 radial at 4,500' MSL or below. When cleared, turn right to right base. Small/light aircraft may request routing over H-1 freeway. Traffic permitting expect clearance via direct Koko Head, direct Waialae Golf Course, then over H-1 to enter left downwind Runways 4/8L. Frequency 119.1.

East Arrival Runways 22/26R— Contact approach control prior to NORBY intersection (MKK 262 radial 20 DME and CKH 112 radial 12 DME) at or below 3,000' MSL. Expect clearance via direct Koko Head direct Waialae Golf Course, thence over H-1 to enter left base. Maintain 2,000' MSL weather permitting (or assigned altitude) until Punchbowl. Avoid flight north of the freeway for noise abatement. Frequency 119.1.

Freeway Arrival Runways 4/8L— Contact approach control prior to Koko Head at or above 2,000' MSL. Expect routing via direct Koko Head direct Waialae Golf Course, thence over H-1 Freeway to enter left downwind to Runways 4/8L. Maintain 2,000' MSL until advised by tower. Frequency 119.1.

Special Note for Kauai Flights— Flights between Honolulu International Airport and the island of Kauai will require the most complex arrival and departure routes of all. Kauai-bound light aircraft will fly either Red Hill Three or West Loch Three departures, depending on runways in use. From the H-1/H-2 Interchange or the West Loch you still must make your way to the west side of Oahu. However, the Waianae Mountains, usually topped with a cloud layer, stand in your way. You may choose to fly north up Oahu's central valley and then west toward Kaena Point, but this route is longer than necessary. Most pilots choose to remain north of the H-1 Freeway and parallel the freeway to the Kahe Power Plant. If you select this route, inform Honolulu Departure of your intentions in order to prevent the controller from terminating radar service too early. Honolulu Departure Control can keep you out of Kalaeloa's airspace if they known your intentions and you work with them. For those segments of flight west of the Kahe Power Plant, controllers prefer to see light aircraft remain north of the Honolulu Class B airspace.

When approaching Oahu from Kauai, remain north of HNL airspace unless turbulence or other weather factors prevent this. A flight outbound on the LIH 105 radial will keep you north. Contact approach control over the Kahe Power Plant at an altitude between 2000 and 3000 feet. From here controllers will advise you to proceed to the H-I/H-2 Interchange. Weather will sometimes prevent a safe flight north of the freeway between Kalaeloa Airport and the Waianae Mountains. In this event, inform approach control of the situation and request an entry into Class B airspace and an alternate route.

AVOIDING COMMON MISTAKES

There's no doubt about it—Honolulu International is a busy airport and can be confusing from time to time. Listed below are two common mistakes and suggestions for avoiding them.

Misunderstood Communications— Frequencies are often congested, and the congestion sets the stage for a pilot to misunderstand a request by a controller. The remedy to this problem is simple: Read back the critical portions of ATC instructions, especially those concerning takeoff and landing clearances. By reading back you not only allow the controller to catch your mistakes, you allow him to catch his own. More than once I have heard a controller clear someone to land on Runway 4 Right and when the pilot read back the runway assignment the controller responded, "Negative, I said cleared to land on Runway 4 Left." We all make mistakes.

Not Clearing a Runway Quickly Enough After Landing— During times of heavy traffic, your slow departure from a runway can cause the plane behind you to make a go-around. Before landing, decide which taxiway you'll use to exit the runway. If you'll be landing on Runway 4 Right and then taxiing to the South Ramp, remember that Taxiway F is used for departures and is normally blocked by waiting planes. A touchdown at the very end of Runway 4 Right when Taxiway F is blocked requires a long taxi on the runway.

YOUR CHECKOUT FLIGHT

All Honolulu fixed base operators require visiting pilots to take a checkout flight before an airplane will be rented. You can influence whether your flight is merely an opportunity for the instructor to examine your flying techniques or whether the flight is a thorough introduction to flying in the Honolulu International Airport area. To make the difference, do your homework and be prepared to ask questions. Study the airport diagram, airport procedures, and approach and departure procedures beforehand. When you meet your instructor, let him know which landmarks or routes you'd like to see pointed out during the flight. Also, show him the flight planning you've done for your trip, and ask him to pronounce the names of enroute landmarks.

A local checkout flight should last between half an hour and an hour. After departing Honolulu International, you'll fly to Oahu's practice area for some airwork. The practice area is bounded to the north by Wheeler Field, to the south by the H-1 Freeway, to the east by the Koolau Mountains, and to the west by the Waianae Mountains. Traffic here can be heavy, particularly near the H-1/H-2 Interchange, so be alert. After the practice area, you'll likely proceed to Kalaeloa Airport (Fig. 5-4 & 5-5) for a few touch-and-goes and then back to Honolulu International. Keep in mind that the instructor must feel satisfied that you can handle the required communications at Honolulu International. The best way to ensure a satisfactory checkout flight is to familiarize yourself as much as possible with the airport and its procedures before the flight.

Many FBOs now require a cross-country checkout before renting a plane for inter-island flight. Typically, a flight to Molokai and return is used to acquaint the visiting pilot with Hawaii cross-country procedures. Communications with HNL approach and island-reporting flight plan procedures are emphasized.

KALAELOA

Many pilots will recognize Kalaeloa by its previous name, Barber's Point Naval Air Station. In the late 1990s, the navy moved flight operations to Kaneohe, making room for general aviation at this airport. The opening of Kalaeloa Airport coincided with the closing of Ford Island to general aviation aircraft.

Kalaeloa is also referred to as John Rodgers Field, a name originally bestowed upon Honolulu International Airport. Rodgers was a Naval aviator who in 1925 attempted the first non-stop flight from the U.S. mainland to Hawaii. When his aircraft was forced down hundreds of miles northwest of Hawaii, Rodgers and his crew rigged up sails and sailed the plane to within a few miles of Kauai. This feat created quite a stir in Hawaii, but over the years Honolulu International slowly outgrew the name. Thus, Kalaeoloa picked up a secondary name to pay tribute to the aviator. Three-letter designator for Kalaeloa is JRF.

The Hawaii Air National Guard provides air traffic control at Kalaeloa, and pilots should be aware that the field also serves national guard and coast guard planes as well. Kalaeloa lies beneath the approach path to Runway 8L at HNL, and for this reason it is particularly important to follow ATC instructions and avoid exceeding maximum altitudes.

Diagrams on the following two pages show arrival and departure routes to Kalaeloa and runway layouts.

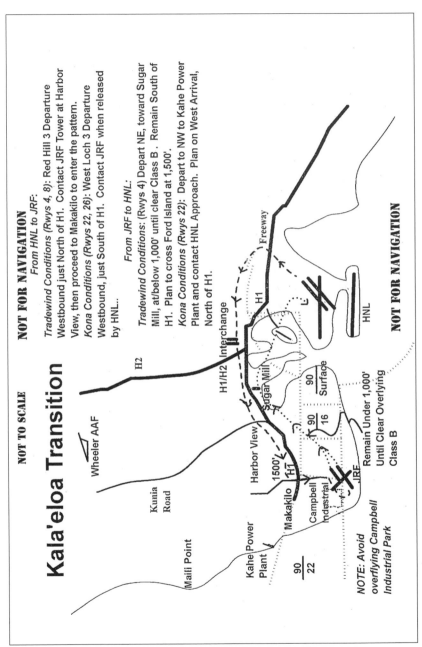

Fig. 5-4. Approach and departure routings at Kalaeloa Airport.

45

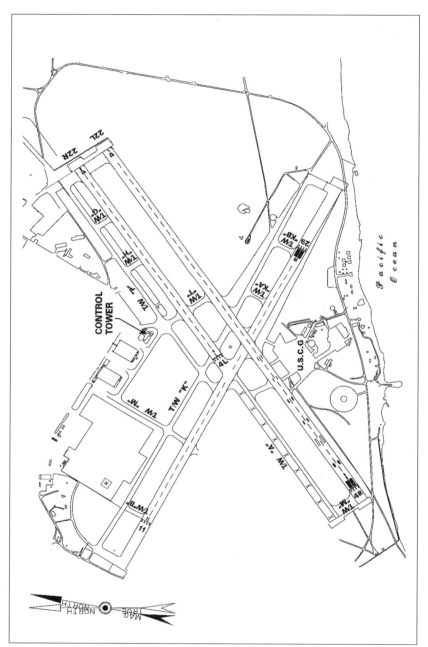

Fig. 5-5. Kalaeloa Airport Diagram.

Chapter 6
Around Oahu

A flight around the island of Oahu (Fig. 6-1) offers more than just an aerial view of Honolulu. From aloft you can enjoy the rugged cliffsides of windward Oahu, the famous surfing beaches of the north shore, and a unique view of Pearl Harbor. The trip is the quickest and least expensive way to see Hawaii from a light plane.

If any of your passengers are apprehensive about overwater flying in a single-engine plane, you can assure them that your plane will always be within gliding distance of land. Many pilots keep a trip around Oahu in mind as plan B. When weather prohibits an inter-island flight, the Oahu trip can sometimes still be flown. If a lunch was packed for that interisland flight, there's no need for it to go to waste, uncrowded Dillingham Airfield on Oahu's north shore is a great place to enjoy it.

Oahu is home for more than 80 percent of the state's residents, and during your flight you may wonder how an island this size can support so many people. Agriculture is part of the answer, and up until recently, great quantities of sugar cane were grown in the central valley and on the north shore. Tourism is an even more important industry, though. The vast majority of Oahu's resorts are found in Waikiki, the most popular tourist destination in Hawaii. Finally, consider the boost given to the local economy by Uncle Sam. All branches of the U.S. armed forces have major bases on this island, and a great number of military and civilian jobs are created directly or indirectly by these facilities.

Many pilots choose to fly their Oahu tours with a flight instructor in the right seat. The money they save by eliminating the checkout flight more than covers the cost of bringing an instructor along on the tour. Financial considerations aren't the only advantage to

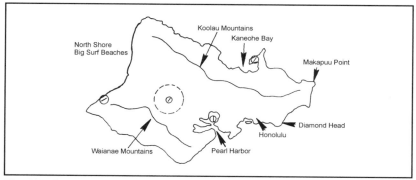

Fig. 6-1. Oahu.

such a plan. A trip around the island requires frequent communicating, at least eleven frequency changes being required, and with the instructor operating the radio you can concentrate on more enjoyable activities such as flying and sightseeing.

The tour described in this chapter begins at Honolulu International Airport and then proceeds around the island in a counterclockwise direction. When tradewind conditions exist, a Freeway Four Departure and an arrival from over the H-1/H-2 Interchange will allow the flight to be conducted without any portion being beyond gliding distance of land. When Kona wind conditions exist, though, the flight should be flown in a clockwise direction with West Loch Three Departure and an arrival from over Koko Head. The West Loch Departure will eliminate the need for a Kona Three Departure and subsequent vectors several miles off Oahu's southern coast.

HONOLULU

Immediately after departing Honolulu International Airport you'll find yourself overflying the city of Honolulu. This is an especially long and narrow city, bordered to the south by the Pacific Ocean and to the north by the Koolau Mountains. With no more land available for horizontal expansion, Honolulu is now growing vertically as high-rise buildings become more and more common.

From aloft you can easily distinguish various districts of the city. Downtown Honolulu, the financial center of the Pacific, is a relatively small cluster of high-rise buildings located southwest of Punchbowl Crater and near the ocean. Just east of downtown lies an area of widely spaced buildings and much greenery known as old Honolulu. Iolani Palace, the only royal palace on American soil, is located here. Near the waterfront on both sides of downtown are the warehouses and other low structures which comprise the industrial section of the city. Up until the 1980s, a pilot could over-fly the Dole Cannery of industrial Honolulu on low-wind days and enjoy the aroma of cooking pineapple.

Waikiki is the most renowned section of Honolulu and can be found towards Diamond Head. As you fly by this rectangular-shaped land of hotels, notice the canal surrounding it on two sides. At one time much of Waikiki was swampland, but the construction of this "Ala Wai" Canal provided drainage and made the land usable.

HONOLULU HARBOR

Honolulu Harbor may not be as famous as Pearl Harbor, but it has played at least an equally important role in the growth of Honolulu. The harbor is located just west of the downtown area and presently provides docking facilities for transoceanic cargo ships, inter-island cruise ships, and a variety of smaller vessels (Fig. 6-2). Much of Honolulu's growth during the nineteenth century was the result of the city's development as a center for trade. Sailing ships could anchor in the protected waters of Honolulu

Fig. 6-2. Cruise ship SS Oceanic Independence rests in Honolulu Harbor beneath Aloha Tower. When Aloha Tower was first built, the building created quite a controversy because of its "great height".

49

Harbor and be replenished with needed provisions. Later, the harbor became important as a location from which agricultural goods were shipped to the mainland. Throughout the Hawaiian Islands, those communities which have flourished are nearly all co-located with suitable natural harbors.

PUNCHBOWL AND DIAMOND HEAD

Many of the world's most beautiful cities can be identified by their landmarks— San Francisco is known for its cable cars and Golden Gate Bridge, Athens has its ancient ruins, and Honolulu has its volcanic craters Punchbowl and Diamond Head. Punchbowl is located near enough to the Koolau Mountains that it receives sufficient rainfall throughout the year to maintain a solid layer of foliage on its slopes. Diamond Head, although just a few miles away, is a chameleon of a crater. Most of the year it is the color of dark lava rock, but when heavy rains come in winter it displays a coat of greenery. Both craters are well-marked on the enlarged Oahu aeronautical chart, and both are commonly used by pilots as landmarks for position reporting.

Fig. 6-3. Punchbowl Crater, the National Memorial Cemetery of the Pacific.

A Freeway Four Departure will allow you to fly directly over Punchbowl (Fig. 6-3). In the days of the early Hawaiians, this crater was used as a hill for placing human sacrifices. Today, Punchbowl is known as the National Memorial Cemetery of the Pacific, and within the crater are buried many servicemen who lost their lives in World War II and more recent conflicts.

Diamond Head is surely the most easily recognized feature in all of Honolulu (Fig. 6-4). Its distinctive sloped shape can be attributed to the work of a strong trade wind which blew ash southwest-

Fig. 6-4. Diamond Head and Waikiki. (courtesy Jim Lockridge)

ward during its eruption. This eruption was a single and short-lived event in which coral from an underlying reef was mixed with the erupting material and became part of the crater. Sailors later discovered glittering coral-based crystals on the slopes and gave the crater its present name. When viewing Diamond Head from its ocean side, you may spot a few bunkers used as gun emplacements during World War II. The guns are gone now, but the crater is still of major importance for civil defense. Within its rim are buildings which house the Hawaii National Guard, the FAA's Honolulu Center, and the Honolulu Flight Service Station.

EASTERN OAHU

After overflying several miles of the big city, you'll likely be ready for the change of scenery provided by eastern Oahu. This tip of the island is much less populated than Honolulu and has taken on some unique shapes as the result of past volcanic activity.

The center of the crater on which Koko Head VORTAC sits is flooded with seawater and is known as Hanauma Bay. Fishing is prohibited in the bay, and as a result the fish have become so tame that snorkelers can swim among them as if in a giant aquarium. North of Hanauma Bay stands 1200 foot high Koko Crater, a volcano with such an awesome appearance that one could easily picture it as a background for a movie about prehistoric times. Eastern Oahu is visited by island residents seeking its fine bodysurfing beaches.

Makapuu Point is the last major attraction before Windward Oahu. Here you'll find an especially beautiful lighthouse and Sea Life Park, Hawaii's version of Marineland. Light planes are requested to remain at least one mile offshore between Makapuu Point and Waimanalo Beach because of extensive hang-gliding activity near the cliffs.

KOOLAU MOUNTAINS

Honolulu is separated from Windward Oahu by the Koolau Mountains. With an average height of about 2500 feet, this line of mountains is able to pull great quantities of rain from passing clouds. The clouds will drop their rain on the Koolaus and then dissipate before reaching Waikiki Beach, a process which is appreciated by both the local water company and sunbathers. Although flying within valleys is an unwise course of action on any of the islands, it is particularly unsafe on Oahu. Many valleys along the Koolau Mountains, especially those near Honolulu and Kaneohe, have high-tension wires strung across them. At one time orange balls were placed on some of the wires to make them more visible to pilots, but nearby residents complained that the balls harmed the view, and they were taken down.

WINDWARD OAHU

Windward Oahu is a great contrast to the Honolulu side of the island. Much more rain falls here, and as a result the land is greener and the cliffs are more spectacularly eroded. The windward side is also considerably less crowded. Once past Kailua and Kaneohe you'll find only small communities along the coast.

From Makapuu Point, the first attraction to pass beneath you will be Waimanalo Beach. It is likely that no other location in the Hawaiian Islands has inspired more songs than this beautiful beach. After Waimanalo, contact Kaneohe Tower for permission to transit their airspace (Fig. 6-5). The preferred route which Kaneohe Tower will request you to follow allows a good view of the Nuuanu Pali, a great cliff abeam Kailua over which Oahu warriors were driven by the conquering army of Kamehameha. Some of the most beautiful cliffs in all the islands are found near Kaaawa. From there to Kahuku Point enjoy the secluded bays and rugged features of this windward side. If your tour takes place on a day when the ocean is smooth, look for giant sea turtles offshore (they appear as small brown dots on the water).

NORTH SHORE OAHU

The north shore of Oahu is surfing country. Along this coastline lie some of the world's hottest surfing spots: Sunset Beach,

Waimea, and Bonzai Pipeline. In summer, local surfing enthusiasts make do with the relatively small waves found off southern Oahu, but in winter, when Oahu is hit with swells generated by storms to the north, surfers head for the north shore. Waves here can reach

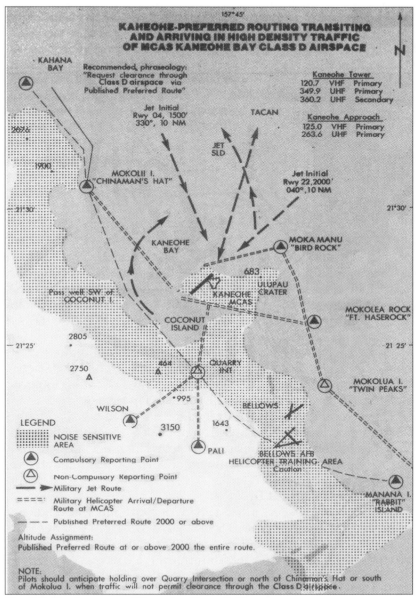

Fig. 6-5. Routing around Kaneohe Class D Airspace.

up to 12 feet in height (measured from the backside; the face is considerably higher). Although surfing is best watched from the ground, you can view the surfers from your plane as you pass overhead.

The north shore of Oahu made aviation history as the site of the first recorded mid-air collision between an airplane and a surfboard. In the late 1970s a small biplane flying low over the ocean was hit by a surfboard and returned to Dillingham Airfield with a piece of the board still imbedded in its wing. The pilot called the local FAA office and filed a complaint about a surfer who had pulled a board underwater and then launched it at his plane. The surfer also called the FAA but told instead how he dove for dear life from his surfboard as the plane approached and that the board must have flown into the air. The pilot had his license revoked for several months because of the incident, a fate much better than crashing into the sea. It is my sincere hope that you remain considerably above maximum surfboard launch altitude while touring the north shore.

CENTRAL VALLEY

Upon reaching the north shore community of Haleiwa, you can continue around the island or turn left and proceed up Oahu's central valley. The central valley route can take you to the H-1/H-2 Interchange in 20 fewer miles than a flight around western Oahu, and if your flight is running late the time saved by taking the central Oahu shortcut can be helpful.

Weather conditions in the valley often do not allow a flight completely above ATC-controlled airspace at Wheeler Air Base, and you should plan to contact Wheeler Tower for permission to transit their airspace by the locations listed in fig. 6-6.

Until recently, Oahu's central valley was used heavily for agricultural purposes. Sugar cane covered most of the valley floor, and near Wahiawa fields of pineapple stretched for miles. Now this valley is supporting a greater number of housing developments.

DILLINGHAM AIRFIELD

Dillingham is Oahu's sport flying airport. On weekends and holidays the skies overhead come alive with gliders, aerobatic planes, and parachutists. These activities take place on weekdays as well, but on a smaller level. The airport is located next to a beach, and if time permits you may want to stop at Dillingham and take a swim in the ocean before continuing your tour of Oahu. An airport diagram and guide to procedures at Dillingham can be found in Appendix A.

The east end of the airport is the domain of the parachuting crowd. Listen for the words "jumpers away" over Dillingham's unicom frequency if you'd like to watch the skydivers in their descents. When departing Runway 8, be prepared to turn left before the end of the runway in order to avoid overflying the drop zone.

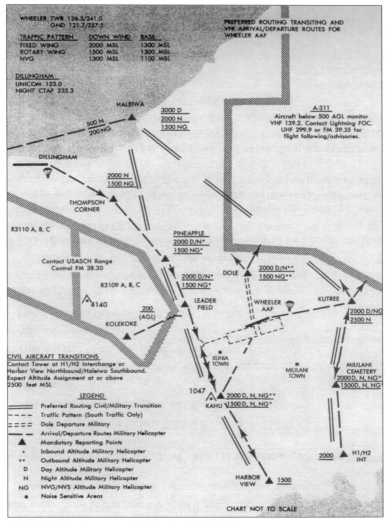

Fig. 6-6. Routing around Wheeler Air Field.

General aviation parking is available on the west end of the airport, south of the runway. A three-story building containing restroom facilities and a pilots' lounge is conveniently located near the parking area. Dillingham's lush tropical surroundings and lack of crowds will allow you to quickly forget that you're on the same island as Honolulu (Fig. 6-7).

Glider operations take place on the west end of the airport, but on the ocean side of the runway. Whether you're a certified glider pilot interested in a checkout or you're just looking for a scenic ride, the local soaring operations can accommodate your needs (see Appendix). The gliders use ridge lift created by trade winds blowing against the cliffs south of the airport.

WAIANAE COAST

The Waianae Coast extends from Kaena Point to Barbers Point. By the time trade winds reach this part of the island, they have already passed over the Koolau and Waianae Mountains and given up much of their moisture. Consequently, the land just inland of the Waianae Coast is the driest on the island and is even susceptible to brush fires after dry summers. The golf courses of Makaha resort area remain green, however. Makaha has been the site of some championship surfing events, and each year a contest is held here in which all surfers must use the long, surfboards of the 1960s, which have now made a comeback. Midway along the Waianae Mountain Range, a highway cuts over the mountains at a spot known as Kolekole Pass. A group of Japanese planes flew through this pass in 1941 on their way to attacking Schofield Barracks and Pearl Harbor.

Fig. 6-7. Dillingham is a great place to park your plane and enjoy a picnic lunch.

PEARL HARBOR

At 7:55 a.m. on Sunday, December 7, 1941, Japanese planes attacked Pearl Harbor. The attack lasted nearly two hours, and when it was finished the 352 Japanese planes had sunk U.S. battleships Arizona, California, Oklahoma, and West Virginia as well as the target ship Utah. Fortunately, our aircraft carriers were not in the harbor and our repair facilities were not substantially damaged. The U.S. experienced more than 3500 casualties in the attack.

As a pilot, you have the unique opportunity to view Pearl Harbor from aloft. As you proceed towards Honolulu International Airport, the standard arrival routes will give you an excellent view of the harbor. Just off the northwest side of Ford Island rests the rusting hull of the Utah. Near the northeast side a line of white pilings marks "battleship row," the docking site for many of the ships damaged in the attack. A white memorial building stands above the sunken hull of the Arizona (Fig. 6-8). The ship's main gun turret protrudes from the water, and its bow and stern are marked by orange floats. To this day, the Arizona will occasionally send up quantities of oil as a ghostly reminder of the event which triggered the involvement of the United States in World War II.

Fig 6-8. The Arizona Memorial stretches above the battleship's sunken hull in Pearl Harbor.

Chapter 7
Molokai and Lanai

If you're looking for a tour that doesn't require a full day to complete, consider a flight around the islands of Molokai and Lanai (Fig. 7-1). These two islands are just a short distance from Honolulu, yet they offer scenery far different from that found on Oahu. The cliffs and waterfalls of Molokai's north shore are regarded by local pilots as one of the finest examples of untouched natural beauty to be seen anywhere in Hawaii. Lanai, on the other hand, offers a view of a former pineapple plantation, recently transformed into a tourist destination. A trip around these islands can provide a great amount of enjoyable sightseeing during a relatively short flight.

Molokai and Lanai are lightly populated, and until recently neither had experienced the rapid growth of tourism that has taken place on other islands. Molokai's few resorts are located on its western coast and near Kaunakakai; Lanai has seen recent developments, particularly in the vicinity of Maneli Bay. The population of Molokai is largely Hawaiian in ethnic background. They're big people, both in terms of weight and generosity, and the nickname "Friendly Island" was properly bestowed upon this island. Most of Lanai's residents are descendants of the men and women who came to Hawaii to work in the pineapple fields. Their island is nicknamed "The Pineapple Island," for obvious reasons.

The tour described in this chapter begins at Molokai's Kepuhi Beach. The route then proceeds along the northern and eastern coast of Molokai, across the ocean to the eastern side of Lanai, and over the interior of that island in a westerly direction. The north shore of Molokai is the highlight of this tour and also the attraction most likely to be temporarily obscured in rain showers. It would be

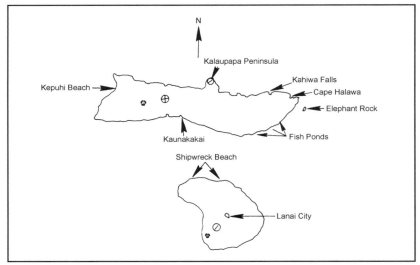

Fig. 7-1. Molokai and Lanai.

in your best interest to begin your tour with the north shore of Molokai so that if weather prohibits your seeing this beautiful shoreline when you first reach it, you can change your tour route and get a second chance to view Molokai's north shore after visiting Lanai. No fuel is available on either island.

KEPUHI BEACH

South of Molokai's Ilio Point lies an uncrowded stretch of beach several miles long. This is Kepuhi Beach, Molokai's most likely location for a developing tourism industry. The Sheraton Molokai is already situated beside the beach, and other resorts will one day follow. You may have already walked upon the sands of Kepuhi Beach without knowing it. Years ago, some of the sand was taken away in barges and deposited on Oahu's Waikiki Beach. If you've walked on Waikiki Beach from end to end, you've surely stepped on some Molokai sand.

Once inland of the beach you'll notice that the terrain below resembles the dry brushlands of East Africa more than it does a lush tropical setting. If you spot a few giraffes or a herd of gazelles beneath your wing, it probably isn't your imagination working overtime; there's a game farm of African animals on this side of the island. Molokai is also known for its hunting. In these remote sections of the island hunters may stalk axis deer or wild boars.

KALAUPAPA PENINSULA

After the Kepuhi Beach area, our tour route swings offshore and parallels the northern coast of Molokai. On a clear day you can view the entire coastline in one glance, and what a sight it is. Before your eyes will be 25 miles of amazingly straight shoreline which looks as though it was shaped by a giant knife slicing vertically through the length of Molokai's northern side. Geologists once thought that the cliffs on this side of the island were the result of a fault line running along the present coastline, but further research has indicated that wave action was the knife which cut the north shore. In either event, after most of the shaping was completed, volcanic activity resumed just off the northern coast and built the Kalaupapa Peninsula.

This peninsula is best known for the work performed here by the Belgian priest Father Damien. In the nineteenth century those residents of Hawaii who contracted leprosy were involuntarily brought to Molokai to spend the remainder of their lives. The isolated Kalaupapa Peninsula became their home, and in 1873 when

Fig. 7-2. Molokai's Kalaupapa Peninsula caught the world's attention when word spread of the work performed here by the Belgian priest Father Damien. Damien's church is the one on the left. The one on the right is Siloama, a Protestant church.

Damien arrived on the island there were some 600 lepers living on the east side of the peninsula. Their community was named Kalowao, and it was here that Father Damien served as resident priest to the afflicted. His mission was to show these people that their God had not forsaken them, even though they had been abandoned by their fellow man. In 1885 Damien became a leper himself, and on April 15, 1889, he died of the disease. For his devoted work with the lepers of Kalaupapa, Father Damien is remembered as one of Hawaii's most inspirational figures.

The old community of Kalowao is gone now, but two churches remain on the east side of the peninsula (Fig. 7-2). The church with the square steeple is St. Philomena Church, and it was built by Father Damien shortly before his death. The church with the Pointed steeple is a Protestant church called Siloama. On the west side of the peninsula stands Kalaupapa Settlement, a state hospital which is home for the area's remaining population of 200. Leprosy is now treated through modern medicine, and residents remain here by choice. The only land route to the rest of the island is a narrow Mule trail above the western end of the peninsula. From a plane you can spot this trail which switches back and forth as it climbs the cliffside. Should you desire to see the Kalaupapa Peninsula from the ground, guided tours are available which originate at Kalaupapa Airport.

NORTH SHORE MOLOKAI

The portion of Molokai's north shore between Kalaupapa and Cape Halawa is certainly one of the most beautiful sights in the Hawaiian Islands (Fig. 7-3). The cliffs here rise as high as 3600 feet above sea level, and there are always at least a few waterfalls tumbling down the cliffsides. After a heavy rainfall the number of waterfalls may increase to well over a hundred. Many aerial visitors to this side of the island wonder why such a piece of scenery hasn't received more publicity. The reason for this lack of attention is simple: No one except a few venturesome sailors and those of us who travel in light planes will ever see this beautiful coast. The rugged terrain and dense jungle growth on Molokai's northern side make the area inaccessible by land vehicles, and airliners fly too high to allow their passengers a good view.

Three large valleys are cut into the terrain between Kalaupapa and Cape Halawa. From west to east they are named Waikolu, Pelekunu, and Wailau. Enjoy viewing these valleys from offshore,

Fig. 7-3. The north shore of Molokai, as seen from near Kalaupapa Peninsula. (courtesy Jim Lockridge)

but stay out of them. In years past the valleys have demonstrated their appetite for light planes.

Besides staying out of the valleys, there are a few other precautions to observe along the north shore of Molokai. Birds fly near the cliffsides, and your chances of striking one increase as you fly closer to the cliffs. An illuminated landing light will increase your visibility to the birds; however, keeping your distance from the cliffs and being ready to turn away from the birds are your two best remedies. Also, keep in mind that the north shore of Molokai is a regular freeway for the state's commuter airline planes. Communicate on frequency 122.9, and make a special effort to spot other traffic, particularly near Ilio Point and Cape Halawa.

KAHIWA FALLS

Most north shore Molokai waterfalls run intermittently, but you can always count on finding Kahiwa Falls going strong (Fig. 7-4). This waterfall drops 1750 feet and is the longest in the state. It Is located between Wailau Valley and Cape Halawa, but even with those directions you can still miss it. The secret of spotting the falls is to look back over your shoulder from time to time as you reach the final few miles of Molokai's north shore. The waterfall is in the back of a short valley, and you need to be slightly east of the falls before it can be seen.

Fig. 7-4. Kahiwa Falls at Cape Halawa.

CAPE HALAWA

Cape Halawa is the name given to the northeastern tip of Molo-kai. As you fly around the Cape, Maui will come into sight, and soon afterwards the island of Lanai becomes visible farther south. The main attraction of the Cape Halawa area is Halawa Valley, located just inland. An altitude of 2500 feet will allow you to over-fly this corner of the island and view the many waterfalls in the val-ley. Be particularly careful to watch for commuter planes that have departed Maui's Kaanapali Airport and are heading for the north shore of Molokai.

ELEPHANT ROCK

The world's largest elephant can be found in the ocean just east of Cape Halawa. This creature weighs several thousand tons and is millions of years old. He's built out of solid lava rock, and when you spot him he'll be lying on his side and enjoying a cool bath in the Pacific Ocean. Aeronautical charts show the lava elephant as an island entitled "Mokuhooniki Island," but pilots usually refer to him as "Elephant Rock." Figure 7-5 shows a view of the elephant taken from the northeast. His trunk extends into the water near the left side of the island, and his tail reaches the water on the island's right side.

EAST MOLOKAI FISH PONDS

A number of fishponds extend into the ocean along the eastern and southeastern coasts of Molokai (Fig. 7-6). Some were built as far back as the fifteenth century, and most were the property of Hawaiian royalty. The purpose of the ponds was to provide the Hawaiians with a ready supply of fish, and there were two principal methods of keeping fish in the ponds. Some of the ponds were equipped with gratings which allowed fish to enter from the ocean but not leave. Smaller ponds could be stocked with live fish during times of good fishing and the fish could then easily be recaught when needed. The fishponds represented an innovative solution to a problem, and one must admire the Hawaiians for building such lasting structures.

Our tour route follows the Molokai coastline until the point named Kamalo and then heads south towards the island of Lanai. The first segment of overwater flight will be above an expanse of coral reefs. These reefs allowed the early Hawaiians to build their fishponds farther out into the ocean that would otherwise be possible, but the reefs also have been a problem for the residents of

Fig 7-5. Elephant Rock.

65

Fig. 7-6. Hawaiian fishponds may be found along Molokai's southeastern coastline. This particular fishpond is located near Kamalo.

Molokai. Nowhere on the island is there a decent natural harbor, and ships approaching Molokai from its protected southern side were prevented by the reefs from anchoring close to shore. The combination of reefs along the island's protected side and the lack of a harbor surely had an adverse effect in earlier years upon the island's development as a center for trade. Today the problem has been solved by air travel and a huge wharf which extends into the ocean near Kaunakakai, Molokai's largest town. You can spot Kaunakakai and its wharf off your right side while heading towards Lanai.

LANAI

When approached from the north, the island of Lanai does not look inviting. Its northern side is pretty much uninhabited and covered with brush. Old shipwrecks protrude from the water near the shoreline. Once you pass south of Kamaiki Point, though, the scenery changes dramatically. Fields of pineapple, more than 15,000 acres in all, covered this ground until recently. Lanai City lies between where these fields once stood and the island's only mountains, and it is shaded by a small forest of Norfolk Island Pines.

During the 1800s several attempts were made at ranching on the island, but with little success. Perhaps the failures of these ranchers helped James Dole buy the island at such a reasonable price. He purchased the entire island in 1922 for slightly over a million dollars. Since that time, the Dole Company's Lanai operation grew to become the world's largest pineapple plantation.

Two often-used bays are located on the island, and each has a major road connecting it with Lanai City. Kaumalapau Harbor is located on the southwest side of Lanai, and most of the island's heavy shipping takes place from here. Manele Bay lies along the island's southeast coast, and it is a popular destination for private sailboats. Less than half a mile southwest of Manele Bay is Hulopoe Bay, a marine life conservation area where fishing is prohibited and swimming and snorkeling are encouraged. Hulopoe Beach is one of the most beautiful in the state, and tourists sail here from Maui's Kaanapali area to enjoy an afternoon in the sun.

LANAI CITY

Lanai City is home for most of the island's inhabitants. Residents here enjoy the use of their own golf course, and they're refreshed by cool breezes which blow through this town located at 1650 feet in elevation.

PINEAPPLE FIELDS

Until recently, Lanai's pineapple fields were the island's most impressive sight to view from aloft. Parallel roads passed through the fields, and trucks with long arms rumbled along the roads and reached all the plants, either for spraying or for harvesting.

The cultivation of pineapples was big business in the Hawaiian Islands through the 1980s, but back in the early 1800s pineapple plants were actually considered a nuisance. Two breakthroughs were necessary before the cultivation of these plants became profitable. First, a type of pineapple was imported that was sweeter and juicier than those previously found in Hawaii. Second, a method was discovered to control the weeds which grew in pineapple fields; a type of paper was laid on the ground with holes cut in it for just the pineapples to grow through. As you fly over remaining fields you may catch sight of shiny sheets of black plastic among the newly planted fields. This plastic serves the purpose once served by the paper sheets.

Because pineapple plants do not normally produce seeds, portions of the pineapple fruit, either its base or its crown, are planted in the ground to begin a new plant. The first fruit is harvested 18 to 22 months later, and it will be the only fruit produced by the plant that is sold whole. All subsequent pineapples grown on the plant will be smaller in size and used for canning or juice. After several years, the old plants are uprooted and new ones are planted. Pineapples were not processed on Lanai; that work was taken care of at Dole's Honolulu Cannery.

Chapter 8
Maui

Maui has long been a favorite destination for visitors to the Hawaiian Islands, and its popularity is particularly great with those who tour the islands in light planes. More pilots rent planes in Honolulu for the purpose of visiting Maui than any other neighbor islands. Perhaps the major reason for Maui's popularity with pilots is its close proximity to other islands. You can depart Honolulu, view the islands of Molokai, Maui, and Lanai, and never find yourself more than 13 miles from land.

Maui is the second largest island in the chain and was created by two volcanoes, one which formed the West Maui Mountains and the other named Haleakala which stands over 10,000 feet high (Fig. 8-1). At one time the valley between the volcanoes was submerged, but through eruptions of Haleakala and changes in the level of the ocean the valley floor has risen above the sea.

Tourism is the island's largest industry, with most of the resorts located along the sunny beaches of southwest Maui. Sugar cane is grown in the island's central valley and near Lahaina, and cattle are raised near Hana in northwest Maui. A fringe benefit of visiting Maui in the first four months of the year is the possibility of sighting whales in the ocean near Lahaina.

This chapter describes a tour of Maui beginning at Nakalele Point and then circling the island in a clockwise direction. Two smaller islands, Molokini and Kahoolawe, can be seen along the tour route, and they're described herein. If your departure point is Honolulu, you'll likely want to combine the Maui tour with a tour of Molokai and Lanai. The group of islands can easily be toured in one day, and this includes enough time for a lunch stop at either Kahului or Hana Airports.

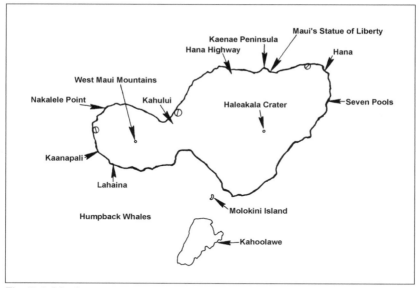

Fig. 8-1. Maui.

NAKALELE POINT

Most light plane visitors to Maui arrive at Nakalele Point (Fig. 8-2) directly after touring the north shore of Molokai. It's a hard act to follow, but the Nakalele Point area usually manages to impress visiting pilots. The shoreline consists of rough lava rocks, and when large swells approach from the north the sight of waves crashing against these rocks can be spectacular. There's even a blowhole along the coast which sends seawater shooting skyward when the waves are right. Toward Kahului stands a huge lava rock named Kahakuloa.

WEST MAUI MOUNTAINS

The West Maui Mountains are the oldest mountains on the island, more than half a million years older than Haleakala, and they're an example of how beauty can come with age. The forces of erosion have over the years sculptured the original West Maui Volcano into the rugged shape of the present mountains. Deep valleys slice through the mountains, and they're part of the reason for Maui's nickname: "The Valley Island." Within these valleys King Kamehameha of Hawaii and his men successfully fought Maui warriors in one of the bloodiest battles of Hawaiian history.

70

Fig. 8-2. Maui as seen from Nakalele Point. Haleakala is the mountain on the left; the West Maui Mountains are on the right side (courtesy Jim Lockridge).

CENTRAL VALLEY

The valley between the West Maui Mountains and Haleakala is a natural wind tunnel. Trade winds accelerate as they squeeze between the two mountains, and the resulting winds blow across the middle of the island with much enthusiasm. Kahului Airport is situated at the north end of the valley, and its reported surface winds typically range from 5 to 10 knots stronger than other airports in the islands. McGregor Point lies at the south end, and the air above it holds the reputation of being the most turbulent spot in Hawaiian skies. Throughout the valley can be found remnants of vast sugar cane fields, and a beautiful old mill is located just south of Kahului Airport.

HALEAKALA

Imagine a mountain so high that its summit tops the clouds and touches the uppermost regions of the sky. Early Hawaiians must have believed that eastern Maui's volcano was such a mountain because they named it Haleakala, meaning "house of the sun."

Legend tells how the sun would rise each morning from a crater near the top of Haleakala and then travel across the sky. The sun made the journey too quickly, though, and the Hawaiian people didn't have enough daylight to make tapa cloth and grow crops. Their demigod Maui, for whom the island is named, decided to confront the sun. He wove together some long ropes, made a noose, and when the sun rose from Haleakala one morning he

71

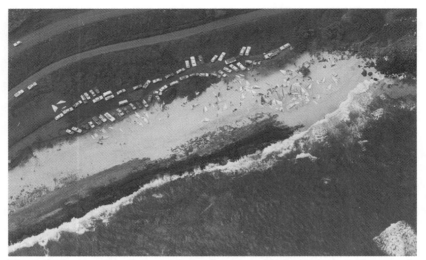

Fig. 8-3. Hookipa Beach, just a few miles east of Kahului Airport. The area is considered one of the premier windsurfing locations in the world. Watch speedy windsurfers cutting through the waves or overfly the beach and view its decoration of multi-colored sails.

snared it. Rather than killing the captured sun, Maui made a deal. In return for its freedom, the sun must travel slowly across the sky part of the year, and this season would be known as summer. The rest of the year the sun could speed across the sky, and this season would be known as winter. Apparently the sun kept its word because to this day the seasons still exist.

If you're willing to climb to 9500 feet, you can take a look into Haleakala Crater. Its floor is covered with cinder cones and resembles the surface of the moon, a resemblance so great that Apollo astronauts were brought here for simulated lunar excursions.

Contrary to popular belief, Haleakala Crater was not created by volcanic activity. At one time Haleakala stood approximately 3000 feet higher than it does today, but stream erosion tore down part of the mountain and carved into its northeastern slope the valley which is known as Haleakala Crater. Two gaps in the valley, Kaupo on the southeastern side and Koolau on the northern side, were created by water running downhill. Only after erosion had dramatically reshaped the mountain did volcanic activity resume, building the cones on the crater floor and sending lava flowing out through the gaps. The last known eruption of Haleakala occurred in 1790, and scientists believe that the volcano may likely erupt again.

Not all of Haleakala's attractions are in the crater. Atop the summit are a group of observatories and other buildings known as Science City. Rumor has it that one of Science City's telescopes was used to inspect the tiles on the bottom of our first space shuttle as it passed overhead.

HANA HIGHWAY

Far below the summit of Haleakala, a narrow road known as the Hana Highway winds its way from Kahului to Hana. The distance between the two communities is only 30 miles as a crow flies, but 52 miles of road is necessary to cover the distance. Along those 52 miles, a motorist will cross 56 narrow bridges and negotiate over 600 curves. He'll be subjected to potholes which are described as "pretty bad" by some drivers and "large enough to swallow a Volkswagen" by others. The speed limit is reduced to 25 mph for much of the highway.

One could expect that the residents of Hana might complain about the road's condition, but this is not necessarily the case. Hana residents enjoy their sleepy town, and they know that a better road would mean more visitors. The Hana Highway prevents Hana from growing like the rest of Maui, and that's good news as far as many residents are concerned.

As you fly along the northeast shoreline of Maui, you should be able to catch a glimpse of the highway from time to time as it emerges from the foliage. The cars you spot on the road will need

Fig. 8-4. Keanae Peninsula.

nearly three hours to reach Hana from Kahului, but you should be able to travel the route in fifteen minutes.

KEANAE PENINSULA

Beautiful Keanae Peninsula can be found seven miles northwest of Hana (Fig. 8-4). Fields of taro cover its surface, allowing an airborne observer to see how Hawaiian agricultural lands must have looked hundreds of years ago. The roots of the taro plants are still used for making poi, but nowadays the finished product is sold commercially rather than being used as a major food source by the farmers. Less than a mile past the peninsula stands Maui's statue of liberty, and you should have your cameras ready for this one (Fig. 8- 5).

Fig. 8-5. Maui's Statue of Liberty holds her lamp high. This natural lava formation is located approximately one mile southeast of the Keanae Peninsula.

74

Fig. 8-6. The quiet community of Hana lies just inland of Hana Bay.

HANA

Both the town of Hana and its airport are magical places. If you spend a few hours at either location you'll likely find yourself forgetting your worries and becoming totally caught up in appreciating the area's beauty.

Hana Airport is an excellent spot for enjoying a picnic lunch. There's a mowed grass area just mauka (towards the mountains) of the ramp where you can sit down and enjoy the scenery. The resident ants in the grass may try to share your meal, but by bringing something to sit on you should be able to overcome that problem. The airport terminal building is open during daylight hours and provides restrooms and a drinking fountain. Activity at this airport is usually slow, and often you'll be able to hear waves breaking on the nearby lava rocks while you enjoy a relaxing moment on the ground.

The town lies just inland of Hana Bay, about three miles southeast of the airport (Fig. 8-6). Hana experienced much of its growth during a time when sugar cane was cultivated in the surrounding area and then shipped from the bay. In the early 1940s the sugar company pulled out, and one of its directors, a man named Paul Fagan, bought much of the land. He used the land for raising cattle and built a cottage-type hotel named Hotel Hana-Maui. The hotel and the cattle business continue to this day.

LINDBERGH'S GRAVE

The famous aviator Charles Lindbergh spent his last years living in beautiful northeastern Maui (Fig. 8-7). Lindbergh was a man who treasured unspoiled natural beauty, and he couldn't have picked a much better spot to find it. The house in which he lived is an A-frame design which stands near a stream with waterfalls. After his death in 1974 he was buried in a nearby church courtyard. At one time several inter-island tour planes would daily overfly the gravesite as part of their tour. Local residents resented having the roar of engines from low-flying airplanes disturbing the otherwise peaceful surroundings, and the tours were rerouted. It would be a shame that a man who both contributed so much to aviation and loved an unspoiled environment would bring this airborne commotion to his neighbors after his death. For this reason, the exact location of Lindbergh's grave is not listed in this guidebook. If you feel a great desire to visit the grave, though, you could rent a car in Hana and ask the rental agent for directions. Otherwise, as you fly

Fig. 8-7. The seven pools of Kipahulu are filled with fresh water and are big enough to swim in.

past the northeastern corner of Maui, dip a wing as a salute to this aviation pioneer.

KAHOOLAWE

Not far south of Maui lies the uninhabited island Kahoolawe. No waterfalls or rain forests are found here; instead you'll discover a desolate island with little vegetation and lots of red soil.

Kahoolawe's forbidding appearance is partially the result of its location. The trade winds which head toward this island must first pass over Maui, and by the time they reach Kahoolawe most of the moisture has already been stolen. Man has also contributed to bringing about this land's demise.

In early Hawaiian history Kahoolawe was used as a prison. Undesirable characters were dropped off on its shores without any provisions. Chances for sustained survival were slim, chances for escape were even slimmer, and a sentence to spend time on Kahoolawe usually turned into a death sentence.

Later on, the island became home for a few hardy ranchers Unfortunately, their goats overgrazed the island's grasses, and permanent damage to the ground cover resulted. Erosion increased and Maui residents began to notice that on especially windy days a cloud of red dust could be seen blowing from the island. The last full-time resident of Kahoolawe left toward the beginning of World War II.

After the war the military took advantage of the island's lack of inhabitants by using it for war games. Since that time the island has been shelled by the Navy, bombed by the Air Force, and its beaches have been stormed by the Marines. The explosions on the island's surface have left thousands of craters and sped up erosion.

In response to the military activity on Kahoolawe, a group of Hawaiians known as Ohana (Hawaiian word for "family") informed the armed forces that some of their members had landed on the island and were hiding out. Shelling was stopped until the trespassers were found and removed to another island. The group believed that Kahoolawe should be returned to the Hawaiian people instead of being turned into a wasteland. The military argued that even if bombing was discontinued, the presence of many unexploded shells near the surface would prevent any future habitation of the island. The military still runs their war games, and the controversy continues.

If you'd like to take a close look at the island, give flight service a call and inquire about the status of the restricted area which surrounds Kahoolawe. If the area is "cold" you can become one of the few visitors ever to view the island in detail.

MOLOKINI

Located between Maui and Kahoolawe is a tiny crescent-shaped island named Molokini (Fig. 8-8). Hundreds of such islands have risen from the North Pacific Ocean during the past few million years only to be torn down by the forces of the sea. Molokini should last longer than most, though, because it is sheltered by Maui from the worst ocean swells. The waters near Molokini are a favorite diving area for local scuba enthusiasts.

LAHAINA

Lahaina is a town with a colorful past. A wide variety of activities have been centered here in the past two hundred years, and whenever one reason for Lahaina's existence disappeared, another took its place.

In 1802 King Kamehameha established Lahaina as the capital of his Hawaiian kingdom. The islands were not yet unified in that year (Kauai was still independent) and Kamehameha wanted a capital which was centrally located. If his rule was challenged on any island, Lahaina would be a good location from which to sail to the rebellion.

The capital of Hawaii was later to be changed to Honolulu, but Lahaina continued to thrive by providing provisions to whaling ships. Between the years 1829 and 1849 more than 500 whaling vessels a year visited Lahaina. The crews of these ships were more interested in enjoying life ashore and replenishing supplies than hunting the humpback whales which wintered offshore. Right whales and sperm whales, to be found farther north, were the primary targets for the harpoons of Pacific whalers.

Since the time of the whalers, two other industries have sprung up in the area. Until recently, sugar cane was grown on the nearby slopes and refined at a Lahaina sugar mill. Tourism has also become important to the Lahaina economy. The town offers restaurants and shopping areas to visitors who stay at the nearby Kaanapali resorts.

KAANAPALI and KAPALUA

The resort hotels of Kaanapali, known for their fine golf courses and sunny beaches, are a few miles north of Lahaina . Years ago, Royal Hawaiian Air Service operated an airport right next to

Fig. 8-8. Molokini Island (courtesy Jim Lockridge).

the beach and brought passengers there in Cessna 402s. Look carefully, and you can still see the strip.

Further north you'll find the resorts and airport of Kapalua. Originally, Kapalua Airport was built by Hawaiian Airlines for use by their DeHavilland Dash-7 planes. The airport turned public years later, but at the time of publication of this book, the airport remains closed to private aircraft.

THAR SHE BLOWS!

"Ahoy! Whales off the starboard wing!" When you spot whales from your plane, really let your passengers know. Summon up your best Captain Ahab voice and sing out.

In Hawaiian waters the king of the sea is the humpback whale. Adult humpbacks average 40 feet in length and weigh about 25 tons. They're the most playful of all whales, and that trait makes them fascinating to watch. The easiest way to distinguish a humpback from other whales is by spotting those long white flippers which can reach nearly 15 feet in length.

Humpback whales are great travelers. They'll spend their summers feeding in arctic waters and then migrate to Hawaii for winters. Whales store up food energy in the form of blubber, and some researchers believe that the humpbacks do no serious feeding while in Hawaiian waters. Instead, their activities in tropical waters are more likely to center upon reproduction. A typical female humpback will mate one winter, give birth the next winter, and rest the third winter. Then the cycle repeats itself.

Here are a few recommendations for sighting whales. Plan your whale safari for the time of the year when whales are most numerous. The humpbacks begin to arrive in Hawaii during November, but your chances of spotting these seagoing mammals are much greater after the first of the year. The whales will remain until mid-April. Look for them in the morning, when winds are most calm. Once the wind speed exceeds approximately fifteen knots, small whitecaps appear on the ocean and camouflage the surface disturbances caused by the whales. You'll find that the white water caused by a splashing whale is easier to spot than the whale itself. As your plane approaches the whale area you may be able to see whales swimming just below the surface as well as those which break the surface. Whales can be spotted near any of the major islands, but they are by far most numerous in the area between Maui, Lanai and Molokai.

You'll want to observe a few precautions while watching the whales from your plane. Check often for other air traffic. When a whale or group of whales is particularly active, the airspace above the activity becomes the most popular piece of sky in the islands. Commuter pilots, air tour pilots, and private pilots all detour in order to overfly the whales. In fact, some pilots even broadcast to their friends the location of the whales. Avoid setting yourself up for a stall-spin accident by paying attention to your flying. Keep your airspeed up, and don't make steep or skidding turns at low altitudes.

A final precaution concerns the whales themselves. They are sensitive creatures which can be disturbed by low-flying planes. Enjoy viewing the whales, but don't remain above one group so long that your presence bothers them and they sound (dive deep underwater). Instead, move on and find another group. To protect whales from harassment, laws have been enacted which require a minimum altitude of 1000 feet for planes circling within 300 yards of whales. If you are convicted of violating this law, you could be sentenced to a jail term or a fine of up to $40,000—and the Lahaina area is home to many individuals who would love to report a pilot for violating this law.

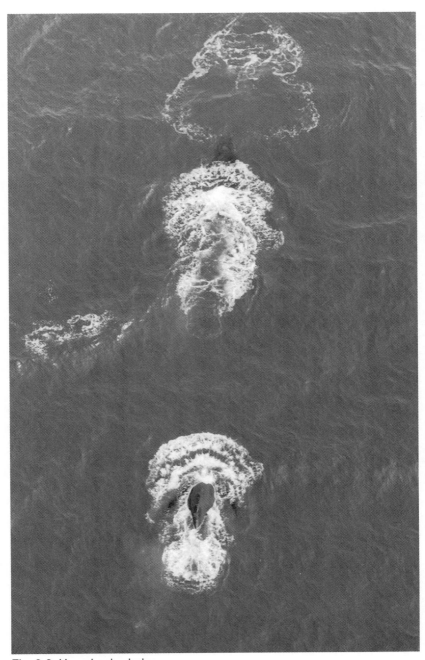

Fig. 8-9. Humpback whales

Chapter 9
Hawaii, The Big Island

If you had to choose just one island to view from the air, you'd be wise to choose Hawaii (Fig. 9-1). This island offers a wider variety of scenery than any other in the Hawaiian chain. Two volcanic mountains, Mauna Kea (White Mountain) and Mauna Loa (Long Mountain), rise from the interior of the island and reach more than 13,000 feet above sea level (Fig. 9-2). Together they form a barrier which significantly affects the island's weather. To the northeast you'll find rain forests, waterfalls, and fields of sugar cane. On the southwest side of the island you'll find the sunny Kona Coast. Add to these sights the steaming craters of Kilauea Volcano Area, and you have an island that is well worth visiting.

Hawaii covers 4021 square miles, making it larger than all of the other Hawaiian Islands combined. The island is so large and diverse in its physical assets that its residents could not decide on just one nickname for their home, so there are three: Big Island, Volcano Island, and Orchid Island.

The local economy has depended heavily upon agriculture. Sugar cane fields covered the Northern coast of the island until recently. More macadamia nuts are grown here than on any of the other islands. Coffee is cultivated near Kona, and the flower industry is big business in the Hilo area.

A typical air tour route around the island requires approximately two and a half hours of flying time. When you consider the time involved to reach Hawaii from another island, you'll realize how a pilot can run out of daylight on this trip. Consequently, if your flight originates in Honolulu, plan on spending a night at either Kona or Hilo. Another good idea is to refuel at Kona (Ke-Ahole) Airport before continuing around the island. Weather on

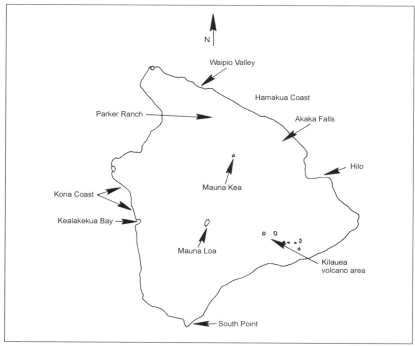

Fig. 9-1. Hawaii, the Big Island.

Fig 9-2. Mauna Kea (left) and Mauna Loa (right) rise above the cloud cover. From this photo it is easy to see why Mauna Loa is known as a shield volcano. (courtesy Jim Lockridge)

the northeast side of Hawaii is often marginal, and you'll be glad you're carrying the extra fuel.

The tour route described in this chapter begins over the northwest corner of Hawaii and then circles the island in a counterclockwise direction.

PARKER RANCH

One of the largest individually-owned ranches in the United States is the Parker Ranch, located in the northwestern quarter of the Big Island. The ranch covers 250,000 acres, nearly ten percent of the island, and extends from altitudes as low as sea level to as high as 8000 feet. Its headquarters is at the town of Waimea, and from here the ranch reaches out in all directions. If you fly inland towards Waimea, you'll overfly such great expanses of grasslands that you may find it difficult to believe that you're in the state of Hawaii. Cattle are raised on these lands, and wherever you find cattle you'll find cowboys. In Hawaii, they're called paniolos, but they carry on many of the traditions followed by cowboys in other parts of the country.

Hawaii's cattle business can be traced back to the year 1793 when Captain Vancouver of the British Navy presented six head of cattle to King Kamehameha as a gift. The cattle roamed free on the island, multiplied quickly, and eventually became a nuisance for the Hawaiians, who knew nothing about controlling the animals. John Parker, a sailor from Massachusetts, was commissioned by the Hawaiian king to round up the animals. For his efforts, Parker was given two acres of land in 1847. Since then, the ranch has been passed down through six generations of the Parker family and has grown to its present size. Figures for 1983 show that the ranch's 135 employees take care of over 40,000 head of cattle.

MAUNA KEA

Just east of the Parker Ranch stands Mauna Kea, the tallest mountain in the world, Quite a few mountains reach higher into the atmosphere than Mauna Kea, but when these mountains are measured from their bases (Mauna Kea begins more than 30,000 feet below the surface of the ocean) to their peaks, Mauna Kea tops them all.

In winter Mauna Kea will often wear a cap of snow at its summit (Fig. 9-3). The snowfall means extra work to those University of Hawaii employees who must plow the road to their mountaintop observatory, but some residents applaud the arrival of snow. Local skiers ascend the observatory road in four-wheel drive vehicles and take advantage of the snow. Better skiing conditions are to be found in Colorado, but where else can you ski in the morning and surf that very afternoon?

If you decide to take a close look at the summit of this volcanic mountain, be sure to monitor Hilo Approach Control frequency while in the area. Pilots of Aloha and Hawaiian Airlines enjoy showing their passengers the snow-covered slopes, and you may find yourself sharing the nearby airspace with a Boeing 737 or a DC-9.

KONA COAST

The Kona Coast stretches along the western edge of the Big Island, and here is to be found some of the finest weather in the Hawaiian Islands. Mauna Loa and Mauna Kea do an amazing job of shielding the Kona Coast from the usual trade winds. On a day when most of Hawaii is experiencing 25 knot winds and broken cloud cover, sunbathers may be enjoying the beaches in the Kona area and windsocks at Kona's Ke-Ahole Airport may hang limp.

To appreciate just how much influence the Big Island's two highest mountains have on the Kona Coast weather, take a look at the ocean offshore Kawaihae on a day when strong trade winds are blowing. Here is the edge of the area protected by the mountains. To the north the ocean will be windstreaked and full of whitecaps, to the south it will be calm. Where the two types of water meet, the ocean surface will toss around in an especially violent manner. Imagine the air overhead behaving in a similar fashion, and you'll

Fig. 9-3. The cones of Mauna Kea's snow-covered summit stand in the foreground; Mauna Loa with its gently sloping terrain can be seen behind.

86

Fig. 9-4. Kealakekua Bay, where Captain Cook met his end in 1779. The lava flow on which he died is the one on the far, left-hand side of the bay. (courtesy Tamra Brown)

understand why Kawaihae is known for its turbulent flying conditions.

Tourism dominates the Kona area economy. Visitors enjoy the comfortable accommodations and sunny beaches found along the Kona Coast. Offshore lie some of the world's finest gamefishing spots, and anglers will journey thousands of miles to try their luck here at catching a Pacific Blue Marlin.

KEALAKEKUA BAY

As you continue down the Kona Coast you'll come across Kealakekua Bay (Fig. 9-4), the site of Captain Cook's fatal encounter with the Hawaiian people. On January 16, 1779, the two ships of Cook's expedition sailed into the bay to take on fresh water and other needed provisions. Their arrival coincided with a festival centered at Kealakekua Bay known as makahiki, and within hours more than a thousand canoes glided across the bay to surround these two ships. The Hawaiians believed that Cook was their god Lono, and he was greeted as that deity. Many provisions were replenished, and Cook's ships departed two weeks later. Unfortunately, several incidents occurred during the stay which soured the enthusiasm the Hawaiians felt for these strange visitors.

The ships sailed north along the coastline until the foremast on one of the ships was broken by severe winds near Kawaihae (this is the same area where light planes usually encounter the worst turbulence of a trip around the island). Cook reluctantly decided upon a return to Kealakekua Bay for repairs. He was not given a friendly greeting this time, and disputes soon broke out between the Hawaiians and the sailors. Captain Cook went ashore with some men to recover a stolen boat and was killed in a small skirmish. His ships and remaining crew continued the voyage.

A white monument marks the spot where Captain Cook died on the peninsula which extends into the northwest corner of the bay. As you fly by, try to imagine how the bay appeared on the day when two sailing ships and a thousand canoes floated upon the water.

SOUTH POINT

The southern tip of the Big Island is commonly referred to as "South Point." Rivers of dried lava stretch down the nearby slopes, and if you look the area over closely you should be able to spot the outline of an old airstrip which served as an emergency field for bombers during World War II. South Point has the distinction of being the southernmost tip of the United States, its latitude being nearly equal to that of Mexico City.

THE VOLCANOES

Hawaii's volcanoes rate as one of the island's hottest attractions. Kilauea and Mauna Loa are the state's two active volcanoes, and they're awesome reminders that our earth is still very much alive and changing. An airborne visitor to the Big Island will certainly want to include the volcanoes in his tour.

When local pilots speak of "the volcano area," they are referring to Kilauea Volcano. Kilauea is located within Hawaii Volcanoes National Park and has been the site of most of the state's recent eruptions. Besides being one of the most spectacular sights to be seen on any island, Kilauea is also one of the most likely to be obscured by weather. Consequently, you'll need either luck or a knowledge of the area's weather patterns to catch Kilauea with good weather conditions.

Mauna Loa is a giant of a volcano. With a summit at 13,677 feet and with more total volume than the entire Appalachian Mountain Chain, Mauna Loa is plenty of mountain. This size creates problems for airborne sightseers. Points of interest are spread over a large area and are at considerably different altitudes. Also, typical rental planes do not have the performance and oxygen equipment required for proper viewing of the summit craters. As a result,

Mauna Loa does not receive as much attention from visiting pilots as Kilauea.

Access to the Volcanoes

Any Hawaiian mountain that reaches several thousand feet above sea level will generate some weather, and Hawaii's volcanoes are no exception. Trade winds bring moist air from the northeast, and when this air rises along the slopes of Mauna Loa, Mauna Kea, and Kilauea, clouds thicken and rain often falls. Rising air is also created when either the windward or leeward slopes of the volcanoes are heated by the sun on warm afternoons. By keeping these two weather-creating forces in mind, you can develop a strategy for viewing the volcanoes.

First, plan your tour to take place during morning hours. Cloud cover and showers near the volcanoes typically increase as the day progresses and the ground warms up. One pilot from Kona Flight Service confirms that whenever he's flying sightseers to view Kilauea, he tries to reach the volcano no later than 11 a.m.

Another idea is to use reported Hilo weather as an aid to predicting Kilauea weather. Ceilings will often differ considerably between the two points, but from these reports you get an idea of the type of weather that is heading for Kilauea. If Hilo is reporting overcast skies and showers, you'd be better off picking another day for volcano viewing.

Choose a route of flight that is likely to give you suitable weather for reaching the volcanoes. The inland and northeastern portions of the Big Island are the areas where pilots most often encounter unsatisfactory weather, and you'd be better off avoiding these areas. To cross the island from west to east, your best bet is to follow the coastline around the southern end of the island. Remain below the clouds and you'll stand a reasonable chance of viewing Mauna Loa's giant lava flows and Kilauea's exotic features. Nevertheless, some pilots will want to overfly the interior of the island, so we'll say a few words about that routing.

The coastline route around Hawaii's southern tip is easy to navigate. Follow the Kona Coast until you are south of Mauna Loa and find your opportunity to proceed eastbound. Then locate the only highway on the southern half of the island, and follow it to Kilauea. On a typical day you can expect to find good weather along the Kona Coast and ceilings over eastern Hawaii adequate for a flight above the highway. The worst weather that you'll encounter will probably be located in the vicinity of Kilauea. Low clouds often extend northeastward from the summit of Kilauea and can obscure some or all of the cones and craters of the volcano area. If you can't view all the features of Kilauea that you would like due to these clouds, you may want to land at Hilo and wait for a change in weather.

A flight across the interior of Hawaii must be a high-altitude flight. The slopes of Mauna Kea and Mauna Loa present a formidable obstacle, and a cruise altitude of 9500 feet will normally be necessary for clearing both the terrain and the cloud tops. When strong trade winds are blowing, a route north of Mauna Kea is best for turbulence avoidance; when Kona winds are blowing, south of Mauna Loa is best. The air between the two mountains is usually turbulent in either instance. If you approach Kilauea from the north or west, you'll likely find yourself overflying a blanket of clouds. Kilauea is located on the 210 degree radial of Hilo VORTAC, and if you haven't reached the edge of the cloud cover by the time you figure that you're over the volcano area, turn south and fly a few more miles. The area just south of Kilauea is known as the Ka'u Desert, and the sky over this desert will often be clear on days when Kilauea and points north are overcast. You won't want to descend through a hole in the clouds which is less than a few miles in diameter, though. Cloud bases often sit right on the ground near the volcanoes, and your descent could set you up for quite a surprise.

No matter which routing you use to cross the island, you'll want to carry plenty of fuel. Pilots will often plan on refueling in Hilo and then be unable to reach that airport due to weather. If you have enough fuel to reach the Hilo area and then backtrack to Kona (Ke-Ahole) Airport with a reasonable reserve, you should be in good shape.

Avoid disappointing your passengers when Kilauea is unviewable by using a technique that some professional air tour pilots have used for years. They refrain from speaking much about Kilauea in the early part of the flight and instead concentrate on giving their passengers a good volcano narration while flying past Mauna Loa or Mauna Kea. Only when these pilots are sure that Kilauea is open do they prepare the passengers for what is about to be seen.

Now that you know how to reach Kilauea, here are two suggestions for departing the area. Most pilots will plan to land at Hilo Airport after viewing the volcano area. A direct flight to Hilo is usually possible, but on days when ceilings are low and rain showers are present, there is a better route. Descend southeastward to the coast, then follow the coastline to Hilo. If you need some assistance in marginal weather, don't hesitate to contact Hilo approach control. Hilo has radar equipment, very little traffic, and the controllers are glad to help you.

Characteristics of Hawaiian Volcanoes

In discussing the volcanoes, we'll start at the bottom and work our way up. Many of the differences between volcanoes in Hawaii and volcanoes located elsewhere are caused by differences in the lava which rises from below the Earth's surface. Hawaiian lava is relatively free-moving and low in gas content, and these qualities are the reason for the non-explosive nature of Hawaiian eruptions. Unlike the eruption which ripped open Washington's Mount St. Helens, an eruption on the Big Island is likely to be gentle and emit large quantities of lava. When islanders learn that an eruption is in progress, many pack picnic lunches and drive until they're close enough to the eruption sight to watch the fireworks.

The shape of a volcano is affected by the ease with which lava can flow away from the vent during an eruption. Mauna Loa and Kilauea have been formed by fluid Hawaiian lavas, and both have taken on wide and shallow shapes. They're excellent examples of what volcanologists call shield volcanoes. As a Hawaiian volcano grows older, the composition of the lava emitted from it changes. A less-fluid, more-explosive lava comes to the surface, and the eruptions build a steep-sided cap upon the top of the shield volcano. Mauna Kea shows such characteristics of aging.

Perhaps the most startling features of Mauna Loa and Kilauea are their rift zones. Not all the lava erupting from a Hawaiian volcano will leave through the top of the volcano. Some will escape through weak areas along the slopes, and these areas are known as rift zones. Rift zones are marked by volcanic craters and cones which extend downward from the summit, usually in a straight line. In the case of Kilauea, some of the points of eruption along the rift zones are as spectacular to view as the summit crater itself. Mauna Loa and Kilauea each include a pair of rift zones, described later.

A variety of dried lavas can be found on the Big Island. Most of the lava found along the slopes is rough and resembles asphalt which has been torn apart by a bulldozer. The Hawaiian name for this type is *aa*. You may spot a smooth, shiny type of lava near the vents of some volcanoes, and this is known as *pahoehoe*. Lava normally leaves the volcano as pahoehoe and then turns to aa as it is agitated and cooled. To determine the age of a lava flow, look at its color. Young lava is typically black, older lava will take on a greyish color.

The more you know about volcanoes, the more you'll appreciate what you see during your flight. If you're interested in researching the subject further, *Volcanoes in the Sea* by Macdonald and Abbot (University of Hawaii Press, 1970) is one excellent source.

Mauna Loa

Mauna Loa is a magnificent volcanic mountain with rift zones extending to the southwest and northeast. When an eruption occurs, it is likely to be spectacular. The following excerpt from Volcanoes in the Sea describes the eruption of 1950:

"At first, two columns of gas, glowing bright orange-red from the reflection of molten lava flows beneath, rose from a point on the southwest flank of the mountain about 12,600 feet above sea level. The eruption point was located on a zone of cracks that extended down the southwest side of the mountain (the so-called southwest rift zone), and during the next few minutes the erupting cracks opened farther and farther downslope. Within 15 minutes the line of erupting cracks was 2.5 miles long, and from it spurted fountains of molten rock (lava) several hundred feet high. The gas cloud rose in a narrow column about 2 miles into the air, then spread out to form a mushroom-shaped cloud brightly lighted by the orange glare of the incandescent lava beneath it."

Fig. 9-5. Kilauea Caldera and Halemaumau Firepit.

Fig. 9-6. Kilauea Iki. Lava shot more than 1500 feet into the air during a 1959 eruption and filled the ajoining lava lake. This photo was taken from an altitude of 1000 feet AGL.

Such an eruption along Mauna Loa's southwest rift zone will usually occur above the 8000 foot level. An interesting variety of cones, cracks, and craters are left behind, but most pilots who view the volcano will see it from an altitude too low to inspect these features. However, lava flows formed by the eruptions are awe-inspiring, and they can be seen from lower altitudes. The area between Kealakekua Bay and South Point is particularly heavy with lava flows.

The northeast rift zone is of interest to both sightseers and the residents of Hilo. If you take a look at a Hawaii aeronautical chart, you'll notice that nearly all of the lava flows from this rift zone proceed toward the city of Hilo. Scientists speculate that there is a good chance within the next few hundred years that a major lava flow will reach the city. If you're considering a real estate purchase in the Hilo area, an airborne view of Mauna Loa's northeastern slope may give you second thoughts.

Kilauea

Kilauea is not your everyday volcano. In fact, when seen from a distance it can hardly be distinguished as a volcano. Its various features lie in low profile on the slope of Mauna Loa, and you could easily believe that Kilauea is merely a rift zone of the larger volcano. Yet Kilauea is very much a separate volcano, with its own source of lava and unique personality. It is characterized by frequent eruptions and spectacular reminders of past eruptions.

Two rift zones extend down from Kilauea's summit. The southwest rift zone has produced great quantities of lava, but the vents from which the lava rose are not particularly scenic. The east rift zone is much more scenic. Kilauea Iki, Mauna Ulu and a chain of craters have emerged from the east rift zone, and they're fascinating sights.

The summit of Kilauea consists of one crater located within a much larger one (Fig. 9-5). The larger crater is known as Kilauea Caldera and it was created when underground lava retreated, causing the top of the volcano to collapse. The smaller crater is named Halemaumau. It has often erupted and spilled lava onto the floor of the surrounding caldera. During most of recorded history, Halemaumau has been filled with an ever-changing lake of liquid lava. At the time this book is written, the crater floor is dried lava, but Halemaumau will surely put on another show before long.

Halemaumau is home for Pele, the legendary volcano goddess. Early Hawaiians believed that Pele controlled all volcanic activity, and efforts were made to stay on good terms with her. If Pele was upset with someone, she would let her sentiments be known through an eruption.

Just northeast of Kilauea Caldera's rim you'll find Kilauea Iki (small Kilauea). One of the most spectacular eruptions in Hawaiian history occurred here in 1959 when a fountain of lava rose skyward more than 1500 feet (Fig. 9-6).

As you continue down the east rift zone you'll come across Mauna Ulu (growing mountain). This offspring of Kilauea has been the site of some of the island's most recent eruptions, and you'll likely find steam rising from its summit (Fig. 9-7). Professional tour pilots will momentarily bank their planes while overflying Mauna Ulu to let their passengers gaze down the volcano's steaming throat.

A chain of lesser-known but interesting craters extends from Mauna Ulu to the eastern tip of the Big Island. When weather permits, a flight above these craters is an excellent way to enjoy the sights while heading toward Hilo.

Remember to watch for other traffic while overflying Kilauea. You may have to share the airspace with military helicopters or other light planes, and their pilots may be as caught up in enjoying the scenery as you are. It's a good idea to announce your arrival on frequency 122.9. Address your calls to "Volcano Area Traffic."

You'll want to be especially alert for other traffic when viewing Kilauea during an eruption. Air traffic over the volcano area

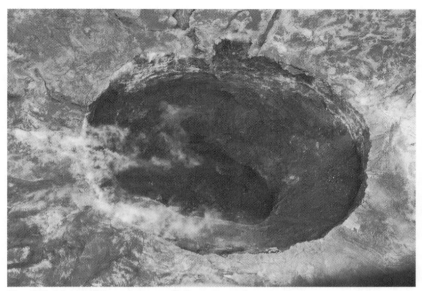

Fig. 9-7. Mauna Ulu— from a pilot's perspective.

Fig. 9-8. Steam rises from the Pacific as Kilauea's lava enters the sea. You can sometimes see orange glowing lava in such conditions. (photo courtesy Lisa Smith).

increases dramatically when an eruption is underway, and special procedures are established to organize the flow of traffic near the eruption site. Your first step for viewing an eruption should be to pick up a detailed briefing from a Flight Service Station concerning the procedures being used. Expect to find a left-hand eliptical pattern in use upwind of the eruption site. Planes are expected to remain clear of the smoke and fly at least 2,000 feet above terrain. A nighttime viewing of an eruption includes additional hazards such as a great potential for spatial disorientation, and such a flight should only be attempted by instrument-rated pilots who are familiar with the area.

HILO

When seen from above on a clear day, this beautiful city appears to have been treated well by nature. The nearby ocean is clear and blue, and the surrounding land is covered with a thick carpet of greenery. Only when you become familiar with Hilo's past, though, are you likely to realize how inhospitable nature can be to such a community.

Hilo is a city threatened from both directions. Tsunamis (sometimes incorrectly called tidal waves) have at times destroyed parts of the city. On April 1, 1946, a tsunami generated by an earthquake near the Aleutian Islands flattened much of the coastal portion of the city and claimed over a hundred lives. Volcanic eruptions and their subsequent lava flows are also a threat. Eruptions along Mauna Loa's northeast rift zone have sent lava flowing toward the city, and someday a flow will probably reach Hilo. Various schemes have been proposed to save Hilo from future lava flows. One of these ideas is to build a huge earth wall uphill from the city that would divert the flow of lava to the side of the community. Another idea is to use aircraft to drop bombs on threatening lava flows and thereby change the lava's direction of movement. The bombing of lava flows has already been tried during past eruptions, and the results show some promise.

AKAKA FALLS

Akaka Falls is notable as one of the most beautiful waterfalls in the Hawaiian Islands (Fig. 9-9). Fed by streams from Mauna Kea, water here plunges more than 420 feet to the bottom of a deep ravine. The main challenge in viewing Akaka Falls is locating it in the first place. The waterfall is hidden among cane fields, and if you don't know where to look, you can miss it entirely.

To find the falls after departing the Hilo area, fly outbound on the 304 radial of ITO VOR until you're 17 nautical miles from the station. Akaka Falls will appear off the left side of your plane. If your plane is not DME equipped, look among the cane fields for a group of trees and a small parking lot. Just beyond them you'll find the falls. A few smaller waterfalls can be found in ravines closer to Hilo, but none of these are as spectacular as Akaka Falls.

Fig. 9-9. Akaka Falls (courtesy Lisa Smith).

HAMAKUA COAST: SUGAR CANE

The gentle slopes just inland of Hawaii's northeastern coastline have previously produced much of the state's sugar cane crop. Fly along this Hamakua Coast between Hilo and Waipio Valley, and you'll see where an almost solid mat of cane fields recently existed. From aloft, the cane looks like a soft blanket of greenery, but remember that you're looking at plants which reach more than ten feet in height.

At any time of year a pilot flying along the Hamakua Coast can view sugar fields at all stages of development. Young cane is green, but as it ages it turns more yellow. About a year and a half after planting, a field of sugar cane becomes ready for harvesting, and it is set on fire in order to burn away those parts of the plants which are unusable for sugar production. The burned cane was then gathered up with heavy equipment and transported to mills along the coastline.

While viewing the cane fields, you'll notice the various crop-duster strips. These had been the domain of the Murrayair. What's a Murrayair? Well, it's the only type of air-plane ever manufactured in Hawaii, a powerful biplane used for spraying chemicals on cane fields .

No discussion of sugar growing in Hawaii would be complete without a few words about the mongoose. In 1872 the Hilo Planters' Association imported 72 of the animals in the hopes that these predators would feed upon the rats which infested the cane fields. Hawaii had no snakes to control the rat population, and the rats each year destroyed millions of dollars worth of sugar cane. There was a major problem with the plan, though: A rat is a nocturnal creature and a mongoose is a daytime hunter. The two animals hardly saw each other. The mongoose population discovered that the small chicks at local poultry farms and the eggs of low-nesting Hawaiian birds were easier to feed upon than rats. Poultry farmers took losses, and several bird species disappeared on the islands where the mongoose was introduced. What had been planned as an aid to the local economy turned out to be an ecological disaster. Fortunately, the mongoose never reached the shores of Kauai, and native birds have survived on that island.

WAIPIO VALLEY

The character of the Hamakua Coast changes greatly as you proceed northwestbound. Instead of agricultural lands which gently slope to the sea, the terrain remains high above sea level until it abruptly plunges to the shoreline. Carved into this rugged terrain is a valley named Waipio (Fig. 9-10). Its steep-sided walls reach six miles into the island's interior. Waterfalls cascade down these walls, and upon the flat valley floor grow fields of taro.

The sharp features of Waipio Valley made this spot a desirable place to live two hundred years ago, a time when the population of the Big Island was divided in allegiance to several different kings. Battles were common, but Waipio Valley could easily be defended. If attackers came by sea in war canoes, their aggression would be noticed because of the limited size of the valley's exposure to the sea. If attackers came on foot, they would have to make the slow and perilous descent down the steep valley walls. Thus the population of Waipio Valley thrived.

Of all the kings ever to rule the valley, King Kamehameha is remembered as the greatest. Known as the lonely one, Kamehameha launched an assault from this part of the island that was to eventually include the conquest of all the other islands. He succeeded through trickery in doing in many of his rival Big Island kings, and then he proceeded to lead attacks on the other islands. Especially fierce battles were fought on the islands of Maui and Oahu. In 1810 the island of Kauai accepted Kamehameha's rule, making this king the first ruler of a unified Hawaii.

Fig. 9-10. Waipio Valley.

Chapter 10
Kauai

Few pilots will dispute the claim that Kauai (Fig. 10-1) is the most beautiful of all the Hawaiian Islands. Fly around this north-ernmost island and you'll discover an abundance of the type of scenery which a tropical paradise should offer. Kauai is more-or-less circular in shape with a 5000 foot mountain in its center and numerous valleys radiating outward. Don't expect to view the mountaintop, though, because it's the wettest spot on Earth and is hidden by clouds all but a few days of the year. Waterfalls plunge from the mountaintop into steep-sided green valleys. Miles of deserted beaches stretch along the shoreline. On the western end of the island lies a huge canyon which shows its red colors when hit by rays of the sun. Nowhere else will you find an island like Kauai.

Besides being the most beautiful island in the chain, Kauai is also the island requiring the longest overwater flight to reach. More than 60 nautical miles of ocean must be crossed between Oahu and Kauai, and on a typical day you will be unable to see land during a major portion of the flight. Obviously, this is not a good trip for individuals who are particularly uncomfortable with overwater flying. To prepare yourself for a Kauai flight, it's a good idea to tune up your overwater cross-country skills by first making a flight between some of the other islands. Several FBOs require visiting pilots to make at least one such flight before a trip to Kauai will be approved.

Kauai is the oldest and wettest of the major Hawaiian Islands. Its lush foliage prompted the island's nickname "the Garden Island." Tourism and sugar production are its two largest indus-tries, and both activities are spread over a large portion of the

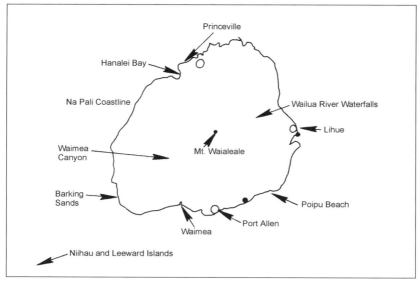

Fig. 10-1. Kauai.

island. Hollywood discovered long ago that Kauai is the place to be for shooting scenes requiring an exotic tropical setting. To list all the movies filmed here would be a momentous chore, so instead you'll find in the following pages the names and shooting locations of only a sampling.

This chapter describes a tour of Kauai beginning near South Kauai VOR and circling the island in a clockwise direction. The tour route departs the coastline near Waimea and cuts inland over the Waimea Canyon before rejoining the shoreline near the Na Pali Coast. A second departure from a shoreline routing is made north of Lihue Airport in order to include the beautiful waterfalls of the Wailua River. The island of Niihau can be seen from Kauai, and information about that island is included herein.

ENROUTE TRAFFIC

The overwater flight between Oahu and Kauai may give you a feeling of being far removed from the rest of mankind, but keep in mind that you're flying along one of the most heavily-traveled routes in Hawaiian skies and you need to remain alert for other traffic. A large number of jet airliners shuttle daily between Hono-lulu International Airport and Kauai's Lihue Airport (Fig. 10-2). For the major portion of the trip, these DC-9s and Boeing 737s travel at altitudes which separate them from light airplanes, but during descents into and climb outs from Lihue Airport they pose a potential hazard for lightplanes. You can take two easy steps to greatly reduce the possibility of a close encounter with one of these jets.

One step consists of simply flying a route different from those used by the jets. If your plan is to circle the island, begin your tour at the southern end of Kauai rather than at Lihue Airport. A flight to the South Kauai VOR should keep you south of most of Lihue's jet traffic, and after circling the island an approach to Lihue Airport from the north will also keep you clear of the traffic.

The other step consists of requesting Honolulu Center to give you VFR traffic advisories. Center frequency for the airspace between Oahu and Kauai is 126.5, and you are encouraged to use the service. Plan to contact Center by mid-channel when heading to Kauai and give Center a call outside Lihue's airport traffic area when departing. Not only will the controllers be able to give you traffic advisories, but you'll be glad you're already communicating with a radar controller should you encounter an emergency enroute.

Many pilots are under the impression that airliners are easy to spot and that radar advisories are helpful only for spotting smaller planes. A jet airliner may be visible at quite a distance when seen from the side, but when the same jet is approaching head-on (as can occur near Lihue) the amount of time you have to see and avoid the jet is minimal because of the small frontal area of a jet and its great

Fig. 10-2. A view of Kauai looking towards Lihue Airport, with Mt. Waialeale in the background. Kauai is free of clouds like this only a couple days each year, and then only for a few hours. (courtesy Jim Lockridge)

closure rate. If you've been alerted of the jet's position, though, you stand a much better chance of spotting it.

POIPU BEACH AREA

A plane on a direct flight from Oahu to the South Kauai VOR will first overfly land near Makahumena Point. Just beyond this point lies a resort area along sunny Poipu Beach. If you circle the island you will see that there are three main resort areas on the island: Poipu, the beaches between Lihue and Kapaa, and Princeville at the island's northeast end. Of the three, Poipu is the only one known for an abundance of sunshine, and residents of the island come here for sun when all other areas are clouded over. The Poipu Beach area also offers some of the best bodysurfing to be found in Hawaii.

From Poipu the next major attraction is Waimea and its beautiful canyon, but you'll find a variety of fine scenery enroute. Most air tour pilots fly slightly inland for this portion of the tour in order to better show their passengers the interior of the island. Below will be a sea of sugar cane. To the right, abeam South Kauai VOR, lies beautiful Hanapepe Valley. Even though it's located on the southern side of the island, the valley is covered in lush greenery.

WAIMEA

Waimea is of interest to airborne visitors primarily because of its historical significance. In January of 1778 the first westerners ever to visit Hawaii anchored their ships offshore the spot where the Waimea River enters the ocean. The ships were the *HMS Discovery* and *HMS Resolution* of the British Navy, commanded by Captain James Cook. Their expedition had begun in England in 1776 for the purpose of finding a seaway between the Atlantic and Pacific Oceans, and Hawaii was discovered while the ships were enroute to the western coast of Canada. Captain Cook saw this discovery as a find of major importance to future travelers and also an opportunity to acquire an extra supply of food and fresh water before continuing the journey north.

Cook and his men made several trips to shore in which they traded iron nails for sweet potatoes, live pigs, and other foods. Unfortunately, certain diseases were introduced to the Hawaiians during these visits which were responsible for reducing the population in the islands from more than a quarter million to only 40,000 within a century. The Cook Expedition visited Niihau after departing the Waimea area and then journeyed north to continue the search for a passage. They returned to Hawaii the following winter, and it was during that visit that Captain Cook met his end on the island of Hawaii.

NIIHAU

From over the Waimea area you'll be able to see the island of Niihau to the southwest. It's a privately owned island with a population of about 250. The inhabitants are mostly pure Hawaiians, and ranching is their principle source of employment. Many of the modem ways of life have been ignored here. The island has no telephone service, no airport, and few modern conveniences.

In 1864 a lady named Elizabeth Sinclair purchased Niihau and part of Kauai for $10,000. She and her children had boarded a chartered ship in Scotland and set sail to find a new home. The tour was to include New Zealand, but King Kamehameha V made her an attractive offer during her Hawaiian stay and Niihau became home. The island's ownership has since been passed down through the family.

Visits to Niihau have been greatly restricted over the years. By keeping down the number of visitors, the residents hope to better preserve their way of life. A flight over this island in a lightplane would not be appreciated by the residents, and you are encouraged to view Niihau from a distance.

LEEWARD ISLANDS

Most visitors to Hawaii are unaware that the Hawaiian Island Chain extends 1200 miles past Niihau and Kauai. The islands to the northwest are much smaller than the major Hawaiian Islands, and most are uninhabited. They're commonly referred to as the Leeward Islands. Some have been completely torn down by millions of years of wave action and only coral reefs remain. Others are barren rocks which serve as home for thousands of sea birds. The names of a few Leeward Islands are: Neckar, French Frigate Shoals, Midway, and Kure.

WAIMEA CANYON

The Waimea Canyon is one of the most spectacular sights to be found on any of the islands (Fig. 10-3). It is nicknamed "The Grand Canyon of the Pacific," and although it is not as deep as Arizona's canyon, it offers sights that can compete in beauty.

The canyon was formed over a period of millions of years as water draining from Kauai's exceedingly moist interior flowed toward the ocean. The water cut deeper and deeper into the island and exposed many of the different layers of lava deposited during the formation of the island.

You can get an idea of the Waimea Canyon's location and shape by examining a Hawaiian Island Sectional Aeronautical Chart. The chart shows the Waimea River extending north of the town of Waimea, and this river marks the center of the main canyon. Several tributary streams are depicted northeast of the Waimea River, and these mark the locations of the side canyons. By then studying the area's contour lines you should be able to piece together a picture of the canyon's layout.

A few precautions should be observed while you're viewing the canyon. Make sure that you've correctly identified the Waimea Canyon and aren't instead flying up a valley that will slope uphill and squeeze narrower. Find the town of Waimea and follow its river up to the canyon. You'll want to overfly the canyon rather than fly in it. Stay over the main portion of the canyon and head northward. Beautiful side canyons with waterfalls can be seen stretching northeastward, but if you fly up one of these you'll be heading for higher terrain and will eventually be unable to stay above the walls of a canyon too narrow to turn around in. Finally, keep alert for other traffic. Helicopter tours are popular on this island, and most of the tours include a flight through the canyon. All island air tour planes reach the canyon in early afternoon, and sometimes several of these multi-engine planes may be over the canyon at one time. While in the Waimea Canyon area, communicate with other aircraft on frequency 122.9. Address your calls to "Waimea Canyon Traffic."

Deciding how to depart the canyon will require some judgment. Normally, when you arrive at the northern end of the main canyon you'll be able to see the Pacific Ocean ahead of you. You then have to decide if the cloud bases are high enough above the ridge in front of you to allow a descent over the side. Keep in mind that quite often you'll hit some abrupt turbulence as you drop over the side of the ridge. If in doubt about this technique for arriving at the northern side of the island, remember that there's a much easier route. Backtrack down the canyon until you find an opportunity to proceed westbound. Contact Barking Sands Tower on frequency 126.2 and request permission to transit the airport traffic area and restricted area. These requests are usually approved. You then rejoin the intended tour route without having hurt your passengers' ears in a quick descent over the northern rim of the canyon.

Fig. 10-3. Waimea Canyon. This photo was taken from a plane heading north above the main canyon. Side canyons to the northeast, such as the one shown here, are beautiful to view but should not be flown up.

MT. WAIALEALE

After viewing the Waimea Canyon, you may wonder how an island the size of Kauai could supply enough water to carve out such an enormous canyon. You have only to look as far as Mt. Waialeale to find the answer. This mountain in the center of the island is the wettest spot on earth. During a typical year more than 400 inches of rain will fall upon the mountaintop, and in wet years there will be as much as 600 inches of rain. The summit of the mountain is nearly always hidden in clouds, and some of the waterfalls plunging down the mountainside give the appearance of originating in the clouds themselves. Less than a mile south of the center of Mt. Waialeale stands Kawaikini Peak, the highest point on the island.

Alakai Swamp is the name given to the shallow-sloping northwest side of the mountain. Great quantities of rain fall upon this piece of high ground, and a wide variety of plants thrive here. The area's water doesn't collect in lakes, as the word "swamp" would imply, but instead flows downhill to form many of the streams found in northern and western Kauai.

NA PALI COASTLINE

Perhaps the most outstanding of Kauai's natural attractions is the Na Pali Coast (Fig. 10-4). Its deserted beaches and uniquely sculptured cliffs give the impression that here is a land far removed from twentieth century Hawaii. The Na Pali Coast is not named on aeronautical charts, but you can identify its location by the dashed red line which appears west of Haena on the charts. To get the best perspective of the cliffs, an altitude of 1500 feet or higher should be used as you view the coastline.

The Na Pali Coast is considered Hawaii's premier backpacking location, and hikers from around the world come here to enjoy the exotic scenery and remote beaches. Look closely as you fly along the coast and you may spot a hiking trail traversing the cliff sides. This is the Kalalau Trail, a heavily worn pathway built by the Hawaiians hundreds of years ago. Part of the trail is a narrow path carved into nearly vertical cliff sides hundreds of feet above level ground. Rocks on the trail become slippery when wet, and the area is rained on nearly every day. Keep these facts in mind as you view the coastline and you'll appreciate your mode of transportation all the more.

Chances are that you've seen the Na Pali Coast before, either in movies or on television. Portions of Elvis Presley's *Blue Hawaii* were filmed here, and a few seconds of the coast are shown in the opening segment of television's *Fantasy Island.* Jessica Lange and a few others walk under a natural archway (located in the foreground of Fig. 10-4) in a recent version of *King Kong,* and in the direction of Hanalei Bay you'll find the location for the filming of much of *South Pacific.*

HANALEI BAY

Hanalei Bay is a favorite destination for those who travel among the islands in sailboats, and on a typical day several sailing vessels can be seen anchored in these protected waters. Perhaps

Fig. 10-4. Na Pali Coastline.

your arrival will coincide with the arrival of ocean swells from the north. If so, look for surfers near the northeast end of the bay.

Aeronautical charts show a river entering the east side of the bay. This is the Hanalei River, and if you follow it for a mile or two it will lead you to acres of taro fields.

PRINCEVILLE

Between Hanalei Bay and the Princeville Airport lies the resort community of Princeville. From aloft it's easy to see that the area's recreational emphasis is on golf and tennis. Vacationers who stay here may not find as much sunshine as they would at other resorts, but they'll enjoy some of the world's finest scenery.

The airport is an interesting sight— that is, if you can spot it. Its single runway is only forty feet wide and was built upon a cow pasture. Occasionally, cows from the surrounding area will try to reclaim their lost territory, and more than once flights from Princeville Airport have been delayed as cowboys on horseback chase cattle off the runway! Princeville operates a unicom on frequency 122.8. Give them a call over Hanalei Bay to announce your intentions of overflying the area.

Helicopter companies launch their tours of the Garden Island from this airport. While lightplanes are fine vehicles for use in touring the island, helicopters are even better. Remember all of those valleys you refrained from flying up because you valued your life? Well, these are all fair game for a helicopter. As passengers listen to a combination of narration and music through headphones, their pilot guides the helicopter into some unbelievably beautiful spots. Imagine the feeling of hovering at the end of the valley with waterfalls surrounding you on three sides. If you're looking for the ultimate view of Kauai, include a helicopter flight in your plans.

WAILUA RIVER WATERFALLS

Kauai's largest waterfalls are those of the Wailua River, and they are about six miles north of Lihue Airport. To reach the falls from Princeville, follow the coast until past the town of Anahola. Along the way you can enjoy viewing a variety of small, secluded beaches. After Anahola, proceed inland over the sugar cane fields towards the Wailua River, shown on aeronautical charts passing south of the town of Wailua before entering the ocean. You'll find the falls along tributary streams slightly north of the main river.

Two waterfalls will catch your attention. The first is that beautiful waterfall shown in Fig. 10-5. The other is named Wailua Falls, and you've probably seen it before. It appears in the opening scenes of television's *Fantasy Island*.

Fig. 10-5. One of the beautiful waterfalls to be found just north of the Wailua River.

Appendix A
Hawaiian Airports

Honolulu International Airport

Elevation: 13'
Runways:　　8L-26R Length-12,357 Width-150
　　　　　　8R-26L Length-12,000 Width-200
　　　　　　4R-22L Length- 9,000 Width-150
　　　　　　4L-22R Length- 6,952 Width-200
Airport Lighting:　　Beacon, VASI: Rwys 4R, 4L, 22L, 26R, 26L
　　　　　　　　　　High Intensity Rwys 8L-26R, 8R-26L, 4R-22L
　　　　　　　　　　Medium Intensity Rwy 4L-22R
　　　　　　　　　　Approach Lights: Rwy 4R, 8L, 8R, 26L

Communications:

Honolulu Tower:	118.1	Departure Control:	
Reef Runway Tower:	123.9	East:	124.8
Ground Control:	121.9	West (low alt):	119.1
Clearance Delivery:	121.4	West (high alt):	118.3
Approach Control:		ATIS:	127.9
(low alt):	119.1	Honolulu FSS:	
(high alt):	118.3	Northwest	122.6
		Southeast	122.2

Airspace:　　Class B

See Chapter 5 for airport diagram and photo

Dillingham Airfield

Elevation: 14'   TPA: Powered Aircraft- 800' MSL
                        Sailplanes-   700' MSL
Runway: 8-26 Length-9,007, Width-75
Communications: Dillingham Unicom- 123.0. All aircraft must contact
          unicom prior to entering traffic pattern and maintain contact
          when operating in the Dillingham area when unicom is active.
Unicom Hours: 0900-1700 local time
Remarks: 1) A 5000' runway for powered aircraft has been painted in the
              center of the existing 9,000' paved area. Powered aircraft
              should use this area as if it were all there is. Do not land short
              of the displaced thresholds. Sailplane pilots will be using the
              first 1500' of the full runway for landing.
          2) Extensive parachute jumping. Jump zones are grass areas just
              prior to beginning of each runway.
          3) Ultralights operating from taxiway, but in contact with
              unicom.
Food & Services : Food, toilets, phones, and picnic tables available.
Airspace: Class G

114

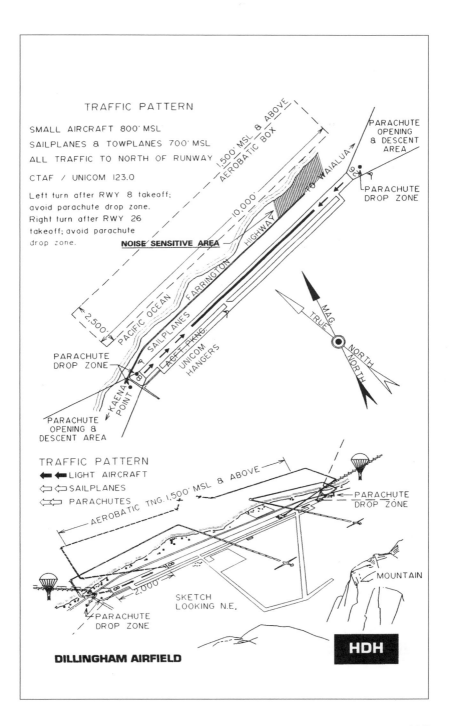

TRAFFIC PATTERN

SMALL AIRCRAFT 800' MSL
SAILPLANES & TOWPLANES 700' MSL
ALL TRAFFIC TO NORTH OF RUNWAY

CTAF / UNICOM 123.0

Left turn after RWY 8 takeoff;
avoid parachute drop zone.
Right turn after RWY 26
takeoff; avoid parachute
drop zone.

NOISE SENSITIVE AREA

1,500' MSL & ABOVE
AEROBATIC BOX

10,000'

2,500'

PARACHUTE
OPENING
& DESCENT
AREA

TO WAIALUA

PARACHUTE
DROP ZONE

PACIFIC OCEAN

FARRINGTON

HIGHWAY

SAILPLANES

ACFT PKNG

UNICOM
HANGERS

PARACHUTE
DROP ZONE

8

KAENA
POINT

PARACHUTE
OPENING &
DESCENT AREA

MAG
TRUE

NORTH
NORTH

TRAFFIC PATTERN

LIGHT AIRCRAFT
SAILPLANES
PARACHUTES

AEROBATIC TNG. 1,500' MSL & ABOVE

2,000'

PARACHUTE
DROP ZONE

PARACHUTE
DROP ZONE

MOUNTAIN

SKETCH
LOOKING N.E.

DILLINGHAM AIRFIELD

HDH

115

Honolulu, Hawaii

Kalaeoloa (John Rodgers Field)

Elevation: 33   TPA: 800' MSL
Runways: 4R-22L Length-8000, Width-200
             4L-22R Length -4500, Width-200
             11-29   Closed
Airport Lighting: Beacon
                   Rwy 4R-22L High Intensity
                   Rwy 4L-22R High Intensity

Communications:
                   Kalaeloa Tower- 132.6 (0600-2200 local)
                   Ground Control- 123.8
                   Clearance Delivery- 121.7
                   ATIS- 119.8
                   Honolulu App./Departure- 118.3

Airspace: Class D 0600-2200 local, other times Class E

Remarks: Coast guard and national guard share the use of airport

Airport Diagram and Arrival/Departure Routings:
                   See Chapter 5

Hilo, Hawaii

General Lyman Field

Elevation: 38' MSL   TPA: 800' MSL
Runways: 8-26 Length-9800, Width-150
           3-21 Length 5600, Width-150
Airport Lighting: Beacon, VASI: Rwys 8, 26, 3
                 Rwy 8-26 High Intensity
                 Rwy 3-21 Medium Intensity
Communications:
        Hilo Tower- 118.1 (0600-2200 local time)
        Ground Cntrl- 121.9
        Hilo Approach- 118.9, 119.7 (Radar available)
        HNL Center App./Dep.- 126.6 (2200-0600 local)
        Honolulu FSS- 122.2, 122.6, 122.1
Fuel & Services: 100 Octane and JetA, some A&P services
General Aviation Parking: Southwest of Rwy 3-21
Food: 1/4 mile walk from parking, or available at airport terminal

Airspace: Class D 0600-2200 local, other times Class E

Kailua-Kona, Hawaii

Kona International at Keahole

Elevation: 47' MSL   TPA: 800' MSL
Runway: 17-35 Length-11,000, Width-150
Airport Lighting: Beacon,   PAPI: Rwys 17, 35
                    Rwy 17-35 High Intensity
Communications:
        Kona Tower- 120.3 (Operates 0600-2000 local time)
        ATIS- 127.4 (0600-2200 local time)
        Clnc Del- 121.9
        Kona Approach- 118.4
        HNL Center App./Dep.- 126.0
        Honolulu FSS- Transmit on 122.1, receive 115.7
Fuel: 100 Octane and jet fuel
General Aviation Parking: Tiedowns available just north of main
                       terminal
Food: Snack bar located at the main terminal
Remarks: 1) Use right hand pattern for Rwy 17.
           2) For taxiway lights when tower is closed, key mike
              five times on frequency 120.3
           3) During the hours when tower is closed, broadcast
              your intentions on frequency 120.3
Airspace: Class D 0600-2000 local, other times Class G

Kamuela, Hawaii

Waimea-Kohala Airport (Kamuela)

Elevation: 2671' MSL   TPA: 3500' MSL
Runway: 4-22 Length-5200, Width-100
Airport Lighting: Beacon,   VASI: Rwys 4,22
                      Rwy 4-22 Medium Intensity
Communications:
              Multicom frequency: 122.9
              Honolulu FSS: Transmit on 122.1, receive 113.3
                      (MUE VOR)
Fuel and Services: None
General Aviation Parking: Find designated spaces on main ramp
                          and use gate SW of firehouse.
Food: None
Remarks: 1) Use right hand pattern for Rwy 4.
          2) Beware of telephone wires 1000' from Rwy 4
              threshold.
          3) Pre-arrange any transportation.
          4) For runway lights, key mike five times on
              frequency 122.9.

Airspace: Class E Mon-Fri 0800-1800 local, other times Class G

Upolu Point, Hawaii

Upolu Airport

Elevation: 96' MSL   TPA: 800' MSL
Runway: 7-25 Length-3800, Width-75
Airport Lighting: Beacon,   PAPI: 7, 25
                      Rwy 7-25 Medium Intensity

Communications:
        Multicom frequency: 122.9
        Honolulu FSS: Transmit on 122.1, receive on
                112.3 (UPP VOR)

Fuel and Services: None
Food: None
Remarks: Activate rwy lights and PAPI by clicking on freq 122.9

Hana, Maui

Hana Airport

Elevation: 78'MSL   TPA: 800' MSL
Runway 8-26 Length-3606, Width-100
Airport Lighting: Beacon
                      Rwy 8-26 Medium Intensity

Communications:
                Multicom frequency: 122.9
                Honolulu FSS: 122.3
Fuel and Services: None
General Aviation Parking: Limited number of spaces available on
                              east end of ramp
Remarks: 1) For runway lights, key mike five times on frequency
                   122.9
               2) Use right-hand patterns for Rwy 26

Kahului, Maui

Kahului Airport

Elevation: 54' MSL   TPA: 800' MSL
Runways: 2-20 Length-7000, Width-150
                5-23 Length-4990, Width-150
Airport Lighting: Beacon, VASI: Rwys 2, 5; PAPI Rwy 20
                Approach lights Rwy 2
                Rwy 2-20 High intensity
                Rwy 5-23 Medium intensity
Communications:
                Maui tower: 118.7 (Operates 0600-2300 local time)
                Ground Control: 121.9
                Clearance Delivery: 120.6
                Approach & Departure: 120.2 North
                                           119.5 South
                HNL Center (for IFR traffic when Maui tower closed)
                         call 119.3 on ground
                ATIS: 128.6
                Honolulu FSS: 123.6
Fuel and Services: 100 octane, jet fuel, maintenance
Remarks: After tower closes, use freq. 118.7 for traffic advisories
Airspace: Class C 0600-2300 local time

Lanai City, Lanai

Lanai Airport

Elevation: 1308' MSL   TPA: 2100' MSL
Runway: 3-21 Length-5000, Width-150
Airport Lighting: Beacon,   VASI: Rwy 3
                     Rwy 3-21, Medium Intensity

Communications:
            Multicom frequency: 122.9
            Honolulu FSS: Transmit on 122.1, receive 117.7 (LNY
                    VOR)
Fuel & Services: None
General Aviation Parking: Room for approx. seven light aircraft
Food: Sandwiches & some food available
Remarks: For runway lights, key mike on freq. 122.9
            3 times for low, 5 for medium, 7 for high

Kalaupapa, Molokai

Kalaupapa Airport

Elevation: 24' MSL   TPA: 800' MSL
Runway: 5-23 Length-2760, Width-50
Airport Lighting: None, runway reflectors for emergency use
Communications:
        Multicom frequency: 122.9
        Honolulu FSS: 122.2
Fuel & Services: None
General Aviation Parking: No paved tiedown spots available.
Food: None
Remarks: Permission is required from State Dept. of Health,
           Honolulu, to enter Kalaupapa Settlement.

Kaunakakai, Molokai

Molokai Airport

Elevation: 454' MSL   TPA: 1250' MSL
Runway   5-23: Length-4494, Width-100
                 17-35 Length-3118, Width-100
Airport Lighting: Beacon
                          Rwy 5-23 Medium Intensity
Communications:
                 Molokai Tower: 125.7 (Operates 0600-1830 local)
                 ATIS: 128.2
                 Ground Control: 121.9
                 Honolulu FSS: 122.2
Fuel & Services: None
General Aviation Parking: A paved tiedown ramp for light aircraft
                          is available SW of main ramp
Food: Snack Bar located in terminal building
Remarks: 1) For runway lights, key mike five times, freq. 125.7
                 2) During hours when the tower is closed, broadcast
                     your intentions on frequency 125.7
Airspace: Class D 0600-1830 local time, other times Class G

Lihue, Kauai

Lihue Airport

Elevation: 153' MSL   TPA: 1000' MSL- Single-engine
                              1500' MSL- Multi-engine
Runways: 3-21   Length-6500, Width-150
                17-23 Length- 6500, Width-150
Airport Lighting: Beacon, VASI: Rwy 21; PAPI: Rwys 17, 35, 3
                Approach Lights: Rwy 35
                Rwy 17-35 High Intensity
                Rwy 3-21 Medium intensity
Communications:
                Lihue Tower: 118.9 (operates 0600-2100 local time)
                ATIS: 127.2
                Honolulu FSS: 122.6
Food: Available in terminal
Fuel: 100 octane and Jet A

Airspace: Class D 0600-2100 local, other times Class E

Photo by Air Survey Hawaii, Inc.

Hanapepe, Kauai

Port Allen Airport

Elevation: 24' MSL   TPA: 800' MSL
Runway   9-27 Length 2460, Width-60
                5-23 Closed
Airport Lighting: None
Communications:
                Multicom frequency: 122.9
                Honolulu FSS: 122.6 or transmit on 122.1 and
                                receive on 115.4 (SOK VOR)
Fuel & Services: None
General Aviation Parking: Limited
Remarks: 1) A fine beach is located near Runway 9 threshold
                2) Right-hand traffic for Rwy 9

Appendix B
FBOs, Frequencies, etc.

FIXED BASE OPERATIONS
Honolulu

Locations: FBOs at HNL are located on the airport's south ramp, which is southeast of runway 4L-22R. From Nimitz Highway, take Lagoon drive towards the airport. All streets will be right turns off Lagoon Drive.

Name: Anderson Aviation, Inc.
Address: 100 Kaulele Pl., Honolulu, HI. 96819
Phone numbers: (808) 833-5899, Fax 833-7437
Email: blankkat@pixi.net
Web page: www.abovehawaii.com
Rental aircraft: Cherokee 140, C-177B, Maule Comet MXT-7-180, C-172RG, Beech D95A (Travel Air)
Availability of life rafts: Yes
Forms of payment: Cash, credit cards, checks
Minimum flight time per day: 1/2 of time away from base must be flight time, no overnights
Reservation deposit: Credit card used to reserve time
Notes: Cross-country checkout to MKK and return

Name: Eveland Aero
Address: 99 Mokuea Pl., Honolulu, Hi. 96819
Phone number: (808) 833-2113
Email: chacy@aloha.net
Rental aircraft: C-152, C-172
Availability of life rafts: Yes
Forms of payment: Cash, credit cards, and checks
Minimum flight time per day: 4 hours
Reservation deposit: 1/2 of estimated flight time
Notes: XC checkout: MKK-LNY-OGG 4-4.5 hrs.

Name: Flight School Hawaii, Inc.
Airport location: End of Lagoon Drive, T-Hangar 128
Mailing address: P.O. Box 6088, Honolulu, Hawaii 96818
Phone numbers: (808) 837-7767, FAX 836-1722, Pager 299-2946
Web page: www.flightschoolhawaii.com
Rental aircraft: Cessna 152, Cessna 172, Piper Aztec
Availability of life rafts: No
Forms of payment: VISA, MC , cash, checks, travelers checks
Minimum flight time per day: 3 hrs. weekdays, 4 hrs. on
                              weekends, 7am to 10am next
                              day counts as 1 day
Reservation deposit: Usually 1/2 of minimum
Notes: Hand-held ELTs available

Name: Kaimana Aviation
Address: 99 Mokuea Pl., Honolulu, Hi. 96819
Phone numbers: (808) 836-1031, (877) 316-2261
Email: acrobat@pixi.com
Web page: www.flyhawaii.com
Rental aircraft: PA-34-200 (Seneca), Cap10 (Dual Only)
Availability of life rafts: Yes
Forms of payment: VISA, MC, checks
Minimum flight time per day: 3 hrs., some flexibility
Notes: Aerobatic instruction available in Cap10

Name: Oahu Aviation Flight School, Inc.
Address: 99 Iolana Pl., Honolulu, HI 96819
Phone numbers: (808) 834-7100, FAX 833-9144
Email: oahuavi@iav.com
Web page: www.oahuaviation.com
Rental aircraft: C-150, C-172, Piper Apache (Dual only)
Availability of life rafts: Yes
Forms of payment: Cash, credit cards (no Discover)
Minimum flight time per day: 4 hours
Reservation deposit: 1 hour deposit over the phone

Name: Washin Air
Address: 100 Iolana Pl., Honolulu, Hawaii 96819
Phone numbers: (808) 836-3539
Email: ogura@aloha.com
Rental aircraft: Piper Archer II, Piper Aztec F
Availability of life rafts: Yes
Forms of payment: Credit cards
Minimum flight time per day: Call
Reservation deposit: Credit card hold booking
Note: Speciallizes in instructing Japanese-speaking pilots

Island of Maui

Name: Airwave Aviation
Address: Building 411, Hangar #108, Kahului Airport, HI 96732
Phone numbers: (808) 872-5688 FAX 871-0960
Email: airwave@maui.net
Rental aircraft: C-172, C-310R (Dual only in C-310)
Availability of life rafts: Yes
Forms of payment: VISA, MC, local checks, cash
Minimum flight time per day: 3 hours, $50 charge for overnight
Reservation deposit: Credit card used to hold a booking

Name: Maui Aviators
Address: Eena Street, hangar 411, Unit 109,Kahului, HI 96732
Phone numbers: (808) 871-6990, (877) Fly Maui
Email: jmuralt@mauiaviators.com
Rental aircraft: Piper Archer, C-152, C-172
Availability of life rafts: Yes
Forms of payment: Credit cards, cash, travelers checks
Minimum flight time per day: 1/2 of scheduled time
Reservation deposit: Credit card required

Island of Hawaii

Kona and Hilo
Name: Sporty's Academy Hawaii
Airport locations: Kona Airport and Hilo Airport
Mailing address: Gate 29, Hilo Intl Airport, Hilo, HI 96720
Phone numbers: (800) 538-7590, (808) 969-2000, FAX 331-2079
Web Page: www.fly-hawaii.com
Email: flyhawaii@fly-hawaii.com
Rental aircraft: C-172, Piper Warrior, Twin Comanche-(dual only)
Availability of life rafts: Yes
Forms of payment: Cash, T/C, VISA, MC, AE, Discover, JCB
Minimum flight time per day: 4 hours
Reservation deposit: Credit card required

EXOTIC AIR ADVENTURES

Aerobatics
CAP10 Aerobatic Instruction
See Kaimana Aviation under Honolulu FBOs

Extra 300L Flights
Acroflight, Inc.
Building 421, Hgr 131, Honolulu Intl Airport
(808) 254-1479

Pitts S2-B Flights
Tsunami Aviation Hawaii
P.O. Box 626, Waialua, HI 96791
(808) 677-3404
Web Page: www.honolulusoaring.com

Float Flying
Cessna 206 Float Instruction
Island Seaplane Service Inc.
85 Lagoon Drive
P.O. Box 30685
Honolulu, Hawaii 96820
(808) 836-6273, FAX 836-7861
Email: seaplane@lava.net

Glider Flying
Grob103, SGS-232, SGS-233 rental & instruction
Soar Hawaii
Mailing Address: P.O. Box 30863, Honolulu, Hawaii 96820
Airport Address: Dillingham Airfield, Rt 930, Mokuleia, Oahu
(808) 637-3147, FAX 637-2360
Web Page: www.soarhawaii.com
Email: info@soarhawaii.com

SGS-126, SGS-233 rental and instruction
Honolulu Soaring
Mailing Address: P.O. Box 626, Waialua, HI 96791
Airport Address: Dillingham Airfield, Hwy 930, Mokuleia, Oahu
(808) 677-3404
Web Page: www.honolulusoaring.com

Open-Cockpit Biplane Flights
Stearman Bi-plane Rides
Mailing Address: PO Box 936, Waialua, HI 96791
Airport Address: Dillingham Airfield, Hangar B6
(808) 637-4461
Web Page: www.peacock.com/biplane
Email: bruceclem@earthlink.net

LIFE VESTS, RAFTS, SURVIVAL EQUIPMENT

Aviation Life Support, Inc.
Honolulu International Airport
90 Nakolo Place, Honolulu, HI 96819
(808) 833-5628

COMMONLY USED VHF FREQUENCIES

Ground Control, Clearance Delivery
Kalaeloa ground control 123.8
All other controlled civil ground control 121.9
OGG clearance. 120.6
HNL clearance. 121.4

Towers
ITO 118.1
Bradshaw AAF 126.3
KOA 120.3
OGG 118.7
MKK 125.7
HNL 118.1
HNL reef runway 123.9
Kalaeloa 132.6
Wheeler AAF 126.3
LIH 118.9

Approach & Departure Control
ITO 119.7
OGG North. 120.2
OGG South. 119.5
HNL App. 119.1
HNL Dep. West 119.1
HNL Dep. East. 124.8

Honolulu Flight Service
Hilo area 122.6
Hamakua Coast RCO 122.2
Remainder of Big Island 123.6
Hana area 122.3
Remainder of Maui 123.6
MKK, LNY to mid-Oahu 122.2
mid-Oahu to Kauai 122.6
North Kauai (Princeville) RCO. 122.3

ATIS

ITO 126.4
KOA 127.4
OGG 128.6
MKK 128.2
HNL 127.9
Kalaeloa 119.8
LIH 127.2

Emergency 121.5

Uncontrolled Field Advisories 122.9

Honolulu Center

ITO area 126.0
OGG area 119.3
HNL east and northeast 124.1
HNL west to Kauai 126.5

Navaids

SOK 115.4
LIH 113.5
HNL 114.8
CKH 113.9
MKK 116.1
LNY 117.7
OGG 115.1
UPP 112.3
MUE 113.3
IAI 115.7
ITO 116.9

HNL FSS Telephone Numbers

Honolulu . . . . (808) 833-8440
From other islands . . . . (800) 757-4469

Appendix C
Exotic Air Adventure

Virtually any type of aviation activity you would like to sample can be found in Hawaii. Have you considered learning to fly float-planes or gliders, or improve your aerobatic abilities? All these activities are available in the 50th state, and you have the benefit of exceptional scenery while aloft. Instead of trying to fit one of these types of flying into your vacation, you may instead wish to build a vacation around your flight activity.

Some aviation activities are specialized enough so that you might not do the flying yourself, but boredom is still unlikely to be a problem. Take to the sky in the front seat of an Extra 300 and experience a lomchevok. Board a helicopter and explore canyons that are too small for a light plane to visit, or feel the wind in your face as you motor along in an open-cockpit biplane.

The activities mentioned below are a sampling of what is available. Business names and contact information can be found in Appendix B. For a more complete listing, be sure to check our web page at www.wecanfly.com/flyhi.

AEROBATICS

Many aviators from the old school believe that a pilot's training is incomplete without aerobatics. There's nothing like learning to recover from spins and unusual attitudes for improving your self-confidence as a pilot.

What advantages does Hawaii offer as a location for aerobatic flying? First, major airports are at sea level and experience moderate temperatures, so aircraft performance should be topnotch for the inevitable climb to altitude. Second, good weather is plentiful. Finally, when learning aerobatics, it is often a good idea to restrict

Fig. C-1. The CAP 10 makes an excellent aerobatic trainer. This one is based at Honolulu International and is operated by talented aerobatic instructor Hank Bruckner.

flying to once a day, not only to assimilate the learning, but also to let your stomach settle down. What better location could you find for entertaining yourself until the following day's flight?

If a complete aerobatic course is too time-consuming for your visit, consider a few flights in a safety course. The beauty of flying in Hawaii is absolutely intoxicating, and the lessons learned could save your life some day.

Looking for the ultimate aerobatic thrill? Consider a flight in a new-generation acro machine such as the Extra 300. Flights are typically short (about 40 minutes) but the newest aerobatic planes have a climb rate similar to a Saturn V rocket, and you waste little time getting to altitude. Basic maneuvers such as the loop or Cuban-8 can be flown with relatively low G forces. Tumbling maneuvers such as the lomchevok can be flown with tolerable G forces, allowing you to experience maneuvers which are the high-light of air show performances. Most of the flying is done by the pilot in command, for obvious reasons, but you will likely be invited to work the controls and do some basic flying, which will allow you to feel the incredible responsiveness of such machines. This is the next-best thing to flying a jet fighter.

GLIDER FLYING

Soaring has been popular in Hawaii for decades now. The reason? Almost continuous lift available from the prevailing trade-

Fig. C-2. Clint Churchill and his Extra 300L at Honolulu International.

winds. Catch the ridge lift along the northeast side of mountains and you can stay aloft almost indefinitely.

On Oahu, the place for glider flying is Dillingham Airfield, on the island's north shore. After a quick tow aloft, you can work the ridge lift on adjacent hills and always stay within easy gliding distance of the field. For mainland pilots who have primarily experienced soaring on thermals, ridge soaring offers a unique alternative.

Your biggest consideration for choosing a soaring day will, of course, depend upon the winds. Enthusiastic tradewinds blow most of the time in Hawaii. Sometimes, though, the trades will be replaced by Kona winds, which come from the southwest, and then the ridge lift is replaced with sinking air.

Fig. C-3. A glider at Dillingham Airfield on Oahu's north shore.

Multiple companies compete for your glider business at Dillingham, so you can expect reasonable rates and a good selection of gliders. They offer rides, introductory lessons, and full rating courses.

You need not leave family members behind when journeying to Dillingham for your glider flights. Picnic tables are available, and vendors sell food at the airport for those who do not bring picnic lunches with them. A nearby beach offers swimming opportunities, and skydiving activity at the airport offers entertainment for those who await your return.

FLOAT FLYING

During World War II, ships dredged the shallow lagoon southeast of Honolulu International Airport to create lanes for seaplane use. The biggest flying boats ever to see active service, the Martin Mars, used these sealanes as they transited Hawaii. Alas, landplanes proved to be more economical for trans-oceanic travel, and the sealanes in Kehii Lagoon fell into disuse.

In the late 1990s an enterprising pilot from Alaska brought his floatplanes down and opened a small business on a floating platform just off Lagoon Drive, next to Honolulu International. Pat Magie has over 27,000 hours of float flying, and he surely rates as one of the most experienced pilots in the business. Pat flies a Beaver on floats for taking larger groups on sightseeing flights around Oahu, and he uses a Cessna 206 for instruction. Expect a full seven hours of flying to complete the course. This certainly is no

Fig. C-4. This C-206 is used for floatplane instruction next to Honolulu International Airport.

Fig. C-5. Stearman biplane along Oahu's north shore (photo by Fred Fujimori).

"quickie" course, but if you're looking for topnotch instruction, consider this option. This business is not primarily a training company and normally should be given a week or two advance notice for training activity.

One of the advantages of learning float flying in Hawaii is that you often have wind to work with. Techniques such as sailing the floatplane can be taught in such conditions.

OPEN-COCKPIT BIPLANE FLYING

If you have never before flown open-cockpit, consider giving it a try. Open-cockpit magnifies the sensations of flight several times over, and when you combine this feeling with the beauty of Hawaii, the experience is unforgettable.

In past years, open-cockpit flights have been offered on Maui and Hawaii. At time of publication, however, the most active biplane business is based on Oahu's north shore at Dillingham Airport. Stearman Bi-plane Rides offers a variety of scenic flights, but they are most known for their Pearl Harbor sorties, which follow a route similar to that flown on December 7th by Japanese attack planes. Pilots get plenty of stick time, if they wish.

HELICOPTERS

Beyond the normal reaches of most visitors lie some of the most gorgeous tropical canyons in the world. Inaccessible by fixed-wing aircraft, many of these Hawaiian canyons include multiple waterfalls streaming down shear rock faces in settings untouched by man. The obvious means for visiting such locations is by helicopter, and Hawaii certainly has plenty of these in daily service on all islands.

The helicopter industry is mighty competitive in Hawaii, so operators have been forced to refine their product. Expect to wear noise-cancelling stereo headsets playing appropriate music during the flights. Years later, when you hear this same music, the tropical scenes will come back to life in your memory.

We pilots typically prefer to handle our own risk-management, rather than trust such a task to someone else. To a certain extent, you have some control over the safety of your flight. Use your meteorological knowledge to choose a lower-risk day for your tour. By avoiding days with strong, gusty winds or visibility restrictions in rain showers, you increase the likelihood of having a safe flight.

For one of the ultimate sightseeing adventures around, give this idea a whirl.

Appendix D
Pronouncing Hawaiian Place Names

Hawaiian is a beautiful language when spoken correctly. Unfortunately, many of the rules for pronouncing Hawaiian words differ from those for English, and a visitor to the islands will likely make mistakes if he tries to sound out the words using his usual rules for word pronunciation. The following guide to pronouncing Hawaiian place names contains the names of those mountains, cities, and other landmarks commonly mentioned during aviation radio communications.

The place names are grouped together according to islands. As a visitor, you should be aware that a few place names are used on two or more islands. For example, there is a "Kaena Point" on both Oahu and Lanai, mountains on Molokai and Hawaii share the name "Mauna Loa," and communities named "Waimea" can be found on Kauai, Hawaii and Oahu.

In the pronunciation guide, each Hawaiian word is divided into syllables, and those syllables requiring the most emphasis in speech are followed by accent marks. The vowel sounds used in the pronunciation guide are as follows:

"ah" as in "father"
"eh" as in "wet"
"oh" as in "oh"
"ee" as in "see"
"oo" as in "moon"
"ay" as in "say"
"ou" as in "loud"
"Y" as in "sky"

Some Hawaiian place names are pronounced with sounds not typically used in pronouncing English words. For example, the final vowel sound in the word "Molokai" is a sound halfway between the sounds produced by saying "ah" and "ee" separately, and the sound produced by just saying -y." To designate such a blending together of sounds, the pronounciation guide shows the desired sound as "ah-ee." On occasion, I have taken the liberty of describing certain vowel sounds in a manner which, although not technically correct, yields pronunciations very similar to traditional pronunciations. Any reader who feels the need to learn how to pronounce all the listed words absolutely correctly should consult a detailed Hawaiian language book.

Whenever an English translation of a Hawaiian word is available, the translation is listed along with the guide to pronouncing the Hawaiian word.

Kauai (Kou-wah'-ee)
Hanalei (Hah-na'-lay): crescent bay
Kapaa (Kah-pah'-ah): the closing
Lihue (Lee-hoo'-ee): cold chill
Na Pali (Nah Pah'-lee): the cliffs
Niihau (Nee'-ee-hou)
Waialeale (Wy'-ahlee-ahlee): rippling water
Waimea (Wy-may'-ah): reddish-brown river

Oahu (Oh-ah'-hoo)
Ewa (Eh'-vah): crooked
Haleiwa (Hah-lay-ee'-vah): house of the frigate bird
Honolulu (Hah-no-loo'-loo): peaceful bay
Kaena (Kah-eh-nah)
Kahala (Kah-hah'-lah): the hala tree
Kahe (Kah'-hay): to flow
Kahuku (Kah-hoo-koo): the projection
Kailua (Ky-loo'-ah): two bays
Kaneohe (Kah-nay-oh'-ay): bamboo man
Koolau (Koh-oh'-lou): windward
Makaha (Mah-kah-hah): fierce
Makapuu (Mah-kah-poo-oo): protruding point of land
Wahiawa (Wah'-hee-ah-wah): place of loud sound
Waimanalo (Wy-mah-nah'-loh): sweet water
Waimea (Wy-may'-ah): reddish-brown river

Molokai (Moh-loh-koh-ee') and **Lanai** (Lah-nah-ee')
Halawa (Hah-lah'-vah): curve

Ilio (Ee-lee'-oh): dog
Kalaupapa (Kah-lou-pah'-pah): the flat plain
Kamalo (Kah-ma'-loh): drinkable
Kaunakakai (Kou'-nah-kah-kah-ee: beach landing
Kepuhi (Kay-poo'-hee)
Laau (Lah-ou)
Pelekunu (Peh-leh-koo'-noo): smelly from lack of sunshine
Waikolu (Wy-koh'-loo): three rivers
Wailau (Wy'-lou): many rivers

Maui (Mou'-wee)
Haleakala (Hah'-lee-ah-ka'-lah): house of the sun
Hana (Hah'-nah)
Kaanapali (Kah-ah'-nah-pah'-lee): the division cliff
Kahakuloa (Kah-hah'-koo-loh'-ah): the high stone
Kahului (Kah-hoo-loo'-ee): the winning
Kihei (Kee'-hay): shawl or cape
Kipahulu (Kee-pah-hoo'-loo): fetch from exhausted gardens
Lahaina (Lah-hy'-nah): cruel sun
Molokini (Moh-loh-kee'-nee)
Nakalele (Nah-kah-lay'-lay): the leaning
Opana (Oh-pah'-nah)
Wailuku (Wy-loo'-koo): water of destruction

Hawaii (Haw-wy'-ee)
Akaka (Ah-kah'-kah): clear
Halemaumau (Hah-lay-mou'-mou): fern house
Hamakua (Hah-mah-koo'-ah): long corner
Hilo (Hee'-loh)
Kamuela (Kah-moo-ay'-lah): Samuel
Kawaihae (Kah-wah-ee'-hy)
Kealakekua (Kay'-ah-lah-kay-koo'-ah): the path of the gods
Kilauea Iki (Kee-lou-ay'-ah Ee'-kee): small Kilauea
Kohala (Koh-hah'-lah)
Kona (Koh'-nah): leeward
Mauna Kea (Mou'-nah Kay'-ah): white mountain
Mauna Loa (Mou'-nah Loh'-ah): long mountain
Mauna Ulu (Mou'-nah Oo'-loo): growing mountain
Upolu (Oo-poh'-loo)

Glossary

Big Island: A nickname for the island of Hawaii.

hurricane: A cyclonic storm originating in tropical regions with wind speeds exceeding 63 knots.

Kona wind: A wind over the Hawaiian Islands which blows from the south, southwest or west. Kona winds are not as common as trade winds.

leeward: The direction towards which the wind is blowing. When used to describe a portion of an island (such as "Leeward Oahu"), the term refers to the island's southwestern side.

Leeward Islands: A chain of small, mostly uninhabitable islands that extend northwestward for 1200 miles from Kauai and Niihau.

makai: Towards the sea.

mauka: Towards the mountains.

mauka showers: Rain showers which occur over the mountain regions of the islands, particularly over Oahu's Koolau Mountains. Mauka showers will occasionally drift leeward of the mountains.

swells: Disturbances upon the ocean surface caused by distant storm systems. Swells are broader and deeper than waves yet often are not as visible during those times of day when the sun is high. Large swells most often occur in Hawaiian waters during the winter months.

trade wind: A wind which blows from the northeast in tropical regions of the northern hemisphere. Trade winds are the most common type of wind found in Hawaii.

tropical depression: A cyclonic storm originating in tropical regions with wind speeds of less than 33 knots.

tropical storm: A cyclonic storm originating in tropical regions with maximum winds between 34 and 63 knots.

waves: Disturbances upon the ocean surface caused by local wind conditions. When wind speed exceeds approximately 15 knots, the waves will break and create whitecaps.

windward: The direction from which the wind is blowing. When used to describe a portion of an island (such as "Windward Oahu"), the term refers to the side of the island from which trade winds blow (the northeastern side).

Index

A

Aerobatics, 137-138
Akaka Falls, 96-97
Alakai Swamp, 108
Arizona, 57

B

Barking Sands, 106

C

Cameras, 4-5
Cape Halawa, 62-64
Checkout flight, 2-3, 35, 43-44
Class B airspace, 36
Cook, Capt., 87-88,104-105
Crosswind taxiing, 6
Cruising altitudes, 20

D

Diamond Head, 49-51
Dillingham airport, 54-56, 114-115
Ditching, 28-32
Ditching statistics 32

E

Eastern Oahu, 51
Elephant Rock, 65
ELTs, 27

F

Father Damien, 61
FBOs, 129-132
Fish ponds, 65-66

Float flying, 133, 140-141
Floatation gear, 26-27
Forced landings, 33
Ford Island, 57

G

Gliders, 133, 138-139

H

Haleakala, 71-72
Hamakua Coast, 98
Hana, 75
Hana airport, 121
Hana Highway, 73-74
Hanalei Bay, 108-110
Hawaii chart, 84
Helicopters, 110, 141-142
Hilo, 90, 96-97
Hilo airport 117
Honolulu, 48-49
Honolulu Harbor, 49-50
Honolulu International, 35-44
HNL arrival routes, 40-42
HNL checkout flight, 43-44
HNL departure routes, 40-42
Hookipa Beach, 72
Humpback whales, 79-81
Hurricanes, 13-14

I

IFR, 12-13
Island Reporting Flight Plans, 17

K

Kaanapali, 78
Kaena Point, 42, 56
Kahiwa Falls, 63-64
Kahoolawe, 77-78
Kahului airport, 122
Kailua, 52
Kalaeoloa, 44-46, 116
Kalalau Trail, 108
Kalaupapa airport, 128
Kalaupapa Peninsula 61-62
Kamuela airport, 119
Kauai chart, 102
Kealakekua Bay, 87-88
Keanae Peninsula, 73-74
Kepuhi Beach, 60
Kilauea, 88-95
Kilauea Iki, 93-94
Kona airport, 118
Kona Coast, 86-87
Kona winds, 10
Koolau Mountains, 48

L

Lahaina, 78-79
Lanai, 66-67
Lanai airport, 123
Leeward Islands, 105
Lihue airport, 126
Lindbergh's grave, 76
Life vests, 26
Lost procedures 22

M

Maui, 69-82
Maui chart, 70
Mauna Kea, 84-85
Mauna Loa, 92-93
Mauna Ulu, 94-95
Molokai, 59-66
Molokai airport, 124
Molokai chart, 60
Molokini, 78-79
Mongoose, 98
Mt. Waialeale, 107-108

N

Nakalele Point, 70
Na Pali Coast, 108-109

Niihau, 105
North vs. south shores, 20
North shore Molokai, 62-63
North shore Oahu, 52-54

O

Oahu, 47-57
Open-cockpit, 133, 141

P

Packing suggstions, 3-5
Parachuting, 54
Parker Ranch, 85
Pearl Harbor, 57
Pineapple fields, 67
Poipu Beach, 104
Port Allen airport, 127
Princeville, 110
Pronunciations, 143-145
Punchbowl, 50
Pyrotechnics, 27-28

R

Rafts, 27

S

Scheduling trip, 2-3
Severe weather, 13-15
South Point, 88

T

Terrain avoidance 33-34
Trade winds, 8-9
Traffic Avoidance, 23
Tropical storms, 14
Turbulence, 20

U

Upolu Point airport, 120

V

Visibility, 10-12
Volcanoes, 88-96

W

Waikiki, 49
Wailua River waterfalls, 110-111
Waimea, 104-105
Waimea (Kamuela) AP, 119

Waimea Canyon, 105-107
Waipio Valley, 98-99
Waterspouts, 14
Weather, 7-16
West Maui Mtns, 70
Whales, 79-81
Windward Oahu, 52